CAMBRIDGE LIBRARY COLLECTION

Books of enduring scholarly value

History

The books reissued in this series include accounts of historical events and movements by eye-witnesses and contemporaries, as well as landmark studies that assembled significant source materials or developed new historiographical methods. The series includes work in social, political and military history on a wide range of periods and regions, giving modern scholars ready access to influential publications of the past.

The Tyranny of the Countryside

Frederick Ernest Green (1867–1922) was a writer who specialised in recording the daily lives of farmers and agricultural workers in the late nineteenth and early twentieth centuries. This volume, first published in 1913, contains Green's description of the poverty and other problems faced by contemporary agricultural workers. Using his first-hand experiences as a member of a rural Surrey parish council, Green discusses in detail many aspects of the lives of agricultural workers. He explains the power that farmers exerted over their labourers through providing both employment and housing, and explores the nepotism that existed in rural local government. Through his descriptions of rural villages and rural labourers' daily lives, Green demonstrates the depressed conditions and lack of social mobility which existed in rural Britain at the time of publication and examines the causes of this, providing valuable information for the study of changes in rural societies.

Cambridge University Press has long been a pioneer in the reissuing of out-of-print titles from its own backlist, producing digital reprints of books that are still sought after by scholars and students but could not be reprinted economically using traditional technology. The Cambridge Library Collection extends this activity to a wider range of books which are still of importance to researchers and professionals, either for the source material they contain, or as landmarks in the history of their academic discipline.

Drawing from the world-renowned collections in the Cambridge University Library, and guided by the advice of experts in each subject area, Cambridge University Press is using state-of-the-art scanning machines in its own Printing House to capture the content of each book selected for inclusion. The files are processed to give a consistently clear, crisp image, and the books finished to the high quality standard for which the Press is recognised around the world. The latest print-on-demand technology ensures that the books will remain available indefinitely, and that orders for single or multiple copies can quickly be supplied.

The Cambridge Library Collection will bring back to life books of enduring scholarly value (including out-of-copyright works originally issued by other publishers) across a wide range of disciplines in the humanities and social sciences and in science and technology.

The Tyranny of
the Countryside

F.E. GREEN

CAMBRIDGE
UNIVERSITY PRESS

CAMBRIDGE UNIVERSITY PRESS

Cambridge, New York, Melbourne, Madrid, Cape Town, Singapore,
São Paolo, Delhi, Dubai, Tokyo, Mexico City

Published in the United States of America by Cambridge University Press, New York

www.cambridge.org
Information on this title: www.cambridge.org/9781108025294

© in this compilation Cambridge University Press 2010

This edition first published 1913
This digitally printed version 2010

ISBN 978-1-108-02529-4 Paperback

THE TYRANNY OF
THE COUNTRYSIDE

In Downland. No room for new cottages !

THE TYRANNY OF
THE COUNTRYSIDE

BY

F. E. GREEN

AUTHOR OF "THE AWAKENING OF ENGLAND," ETC.

WITH TWELVE ILLUSTRATIONS

T. FISHER UNWIN
LONDON: ADELPHI TERRACE
LEIPSIC: INSELSTRASSE 20

FIRST PUBLISHED, 1913

THE MAN WITH THE HOE

God made man in His own image, in the image of God made
He him.—GENESIS.

> *Bowed by the weight of centuries he leans*
> *Upon his hoe and gazes on the ground,*
> *The emptiness of ages in his face,*
> *And on his back the burden of the world.*
> *Who made him dead to rapture and despair,*
> *A thing that grieves not and that never hopes,*
> *Stolid and stunned, a brother to the ox ?*
> *Who loosened and let down this brutal jaw ?*
> *Whose was the hand that slanted back this brow ?*
> *Whose breath blew out the light within this brain ?*
> *Is this the Thing the Lord God made and gave*
> *To have dominion over sea and land ;*
> *To trace the stars and search the heavens for power ;*
> *To feel the passion of Eternity ?*
> *Is this the dream He dreamed who shaped the suns*
> *And pillared the blue firmament with light ?*
> *Down all the stretch of Hell to its last gulf*
> *There is no shape more terrible than this,*
> *More filled with signs and portents for the soul,*
> *More fraught with menace to the universe.*
>
> *What gulfs between him and the seraphim !*
> *Slave of the wheel of labour, what to him*
> *Are Plato and the swing of Pleiades ?*
> *What the long reaches of the peaks of song,*
> *The rift of dawn, the reddening of the rose ?*
> *Through this dread shape the suffering ages look ;*
> *Time's tragedy is in that aching stoop ;*
> *Through this dread shape humanity betrayed,*
> *Plundered, profaned and disinherited,*
> *Cries protest to the Judges of the World,*
> *A protest that is also prophecy.*

O masters, lords and rulers in all lands,
Is this the handiwork you give to God,
This monstrous thing distorted and soul-quenched?
How will you ever straighten up this shape ;
Touch it again with immortality ;
Give back the upward looking and the light ;
Rebuild in it the music and the dream ;
Make right the immemorial infamies,
Perfidious wrongs, immedicable woes ?

O masters, lords and rulers in all lands,
How will the future reckon with this Man ?
How answer his brute question in that hour
When whirlwinds of rebellion shake the world ?
How will it be with kingdoms and with kings,
With those who shaped him to the thing he is,
When this dumb Terror shall reply to God,
After the silence of the centuries ?

                                        EDWIN MARKHAM.

CONTENTS

vii

CONTENTS

LIST OF ILLUSTRATIONS

It is almost impossible to estimate a land-owner's power. Outsiders imagine it is curtailed in these democratic days, I know otherwise. The landowner has the farmers in his grip, and they are aware of it, and grovel before him. Through them he controls the ploughmen. The villagers as well are in his hands; they work for him or his tenants; they occupy houses owned by him or his dependents. Even the higher-class resident, the doctor, the schoolmaster, the shopkeeper, dare not oppose the laird. A word from him or his factor and their custom would be gone.

.   .   .   .

I should say indeed that never in history has his power been greater than it is now.— JAMES BRYCE, in *The Story of a Ploughboy*.

THE TYRANNY OF
THE COUNTRYSIDE

CHAPTER I

THE PROLOGUE

SIR ARTHUR QUILLER COUCH declared in
Public Opinion that, in performing his duties
as a County Councillor of Cornwall, he found,
when passing from the town to the country,
he passed from the homes of the free to the
homes of the unfree. "Furthermore," he
added, "I regret to have to put it brutally,
but if you really want to know where, in my
opinion, lies England's one chance of re-
gaining her alleged pride in a bold peasantry,
I answer, 'In the bold peasantry having
the boldness to organise a strike.'"

Now, no one could accuse "Q" of being a
syndicalist, and yet his assertion leads one
to suppose that he regards Parliament as an
instrument too slow in its action for bettering
the conditions of the agricultural labourer;

and the utterances in the article referred to, instead of being expressed by a distinguished novelist, might surely have been taken from a speech by Mr. Tom Mann !

Fortunately, or unfortunately, a general strike amongst labourers is little likely to take place, for though our peasantry is still our largest class, it is certainly the worst organised. It is a class which is not vocal. It is a class which has not a single representative in Parliament. The peasant does not organise ; he does not strike. If he can manage to escape unburdened by debt or family, he quietly knots his red handkerchief, and sullenly sets his face towards that lurid light in the sky, which at nightfall betokens the town with its compelling lure of a life of greater freedom.

If he be young and lusty, and has a few golden coins to jingle in his pocket, he may escape altogether from the Mother Country and renounce his nationality. If he be a youth who is walking out with his lass, he too is to be seen setting his face towards the town ; for as cottages tumble down or are compulsorily closed, he will have to seek a roof for himself and his future wife, where chimneys are closer together, and where even the jerry-builder is joyously hailed as a philanthropist. On his way out of the village he may pass the Village Institute, and in spite of its warm, friendly, red blinds, its bagatelle table, its library of sermons and sporting journals, its pictures of saints, of crowned heads and of politicians, he will probably shake the dust of his native village from his iron-shod boots without regret. He wants a cottage, and no landlord or public body will build it. He wants, too, better wages: 12s., 15s., or even 18s. a week is not good enough, he avers, to look forward to, nor a sum large enough on which to found and nourish an Imperial Race. Above all he wants greater freedom. He seeks a place where he can meet many others like himself on terms of comradeship, some place where the eye of his employer-landlord is not always upon him, during his leisure as well as his working hours.

If he be middle-aged and have a wife and five or six children living under a roof, let to him by his employer; if there be no money wherewith to pay his removal expenses, let alone squaring up with the village tradesmen, he must remain a crushed, disheartened, lifeless man, a thrall with nothing to look forward to but a dreary life of unremitting toil, unrelieved by festivals or Holy Days. So he stays and becomes the man whose portrait is seared for ever on our con-

sciences in the burning words of Edwin
Markham :

> Bowed by the weight of centuries he leans
> Upon his hoe and gazes on the ground,
> The emptiness of ages in his face,
> And on his back the burden of the world.

Yet is it not possible that the agricultural
labourer may strike ? History has an odd
trick of repeating herself. It may be that
some day we shall awake to learn that the
most patient, the most docile, and the most
stubborn of all the workers who supply us
with our daily bread has at last been stung
into open revolt.

He broke into revolt in 1830, and the
revolt with alarming rapidity spread over
the Southern and Midland counties like a
prairie fire, though these were the days
before the telegraph wire, the steam engine,
and the capable trade union organiser.

In 1795 his wife, unable to get food for her
children, broke into a still more remarkable
revolt. Simultaneously, in counties as far
apart as Nottingham and Gloucester, labourers' wives commandeered millers' carts and
butchers' shops, and even held up a ship
about to set sail from Bristol, filled with
grain reaped from the fields that they had
gleaned.

To-day, a general strike amongst labourers

should be easier to organise if the great industrial trade unions directed the revolt. But if it were ever brought about, it would become something more than a strike—the nation would be riven in two. And if perchance the peasant class were broken in pieces, we should have destroyed the greatest artery that nourishes the heart of our Empire. Should it drift, as a class, from the open fields into the fetid slums of our towns to seek the greater freedom to be found there, our unique place as a maritime Power would be doomed. Doctors tell us that, after three generations, born-and-bred cockneys become sterile. It is the despised yokel who rejuvenates our cities, who recruits our army, who mans our ships of war. There is a Russian saying that the peasant " must be boiled in the factory pot before a revolution can succeed." Though the English village labourer enters no factory, his son does; and when once the Jolly Roger is hoisted the Red Ensign will dip to it.

That there is a social unrest in our fields as well as in our factories who can doubt ? That it is reticent and does not flaunt itself, does not behave itself unseemly, is not easily provoked, but endureth all things —*that* does not prove that there is no unrest. Is it not written that the meek shall

inherit the earth ? It is true that no
words of burning oratory spring from the
lips of Members of Parliament about the
life of the peasant ; it is true that no single
organ proclaims the wrongs of the village
labourer ; nevertheless the evidence lies
startlingly revealed to all those who have
eyes to see—in the empty and silent places
of our countryside. Hodge works as an
isolated unit in the midst of large and lonely
fields, and it is only when an eviction takes
place that the ordinary citizen awakens to
the fact that he might be living in another
Emerald Isle.

Such an eviction took place on January 21
of this year, and set everyone in Wiltshire
thinking, when at Foxham, with snow upon
the ground, several cottagers with their
families were turned out of their homes on
to the roadside. Also when, in the following
month, a landlord in the adjoining county
evicted tenants for complaining of the want
of cottage accommodation. He was, though,
merely following the example set by public
bodies. If there were a housing problem,
he must either let it settle itself—a plan
much favoured by the Local Government Board—by waiting until the overcrowded denizens had drifted into towns,
or adopt a method prevalent in the Middle

Ages, and known as " decanting "—that is, to tell the people they were too thick upon the ground, rendering cottages insanitary, and that those who were not required to do service on the owner's estate must seek fresh fields and pastures new.

It will now have been made clear, I think, that the tyranny I am about to describe is something deeper-rooted in peasant life than the tyranny of political intimidation over which Liberal orators wax eloquent at election time—especially if a Conservative happens to get elected. We hear very little about political intimidation when a Liberal candidate gets elected in a constituency where a Whig family is territorially strong. The tyranny I speak about is economic rather than political. Political tyranny is only possible because it has behind it the pressure of the economic screw. Political tyranny is sporadic ; quinquennial. It is the tyranny which endures long after the wave of political passion has passed that I shall attempt to describe.

If one of the governing classes is to be indicted rather than another, it is certainly the large farmer class.

For if rural England was once ruled by its magistracy, to-day it is ruled by the large farmers ; and it is this class more than any

2

other which is bringing about its decay. Perhaps, though, it would be hard to say whether it is the large farmer, in his desire to add field to field and to prevent the agricultural labourer from getting land or living in cottages independent of him as landlord ; or the large landowner, in his insatiable lust to obtain huge pheasant-preserves, vast deer forests, and multitudinous rabbit-warrens, who has done the greater harm to our most virile class of workers, and through them struck a blow at the heart of our Empire.

The demon of political intimidation is always one difficult to scotch. It has often evaded both political parties in the Law Courts. It is as elusive, as intangible, as a ghost. Nevertheless, it is as real as a ghost to those who fear retribution from some unseen power. Most political magnates are clever enough to cast the shadow of fear over the mind of the labouring poor without showing the hand of flesh that throws the shadow. Few adopt the rude method of a village publican known to me who said to a labourer, " If you don't vote for so-and-so we'll make it hot for you in this village " ; and few are as stupid as a millionaire in a neighbouring parish, who stated in print that, if the Budget candidate were elected, he would have to reduce his staff of chauffeurs, gardeners, and footmen. The Budget was passed, however, and strange to say this millionaire has exactly the same number of servants as he had before !

Political intimidation cuts both ways. I have attended Liberal meetings in the country where I have seen Tory coachmen lustily singing Radical songs of freedom under the approving eye of their Liberal mistress who sat upon the platform.

Recently, I visited a little country town where there is practically only one employer of labour. He employs two thousand hands in his factory and he is a Liberal. I called upon one of his employees, who, I was told, was interested in small holdings. " Do you mind speaking to me outside," said this free Briton who flew the Liberal colours. " The Guvnor's all right, you know, but as he owns twenty-five farms and most of the cottages in the town, he does not approve of the Small Holdings Act, nor of the Housing Act, nor of the Insurance Act ! "

Now you may tell Hodge that he is better off than his grandfather was. You may tell him that his great-grandfather lived in a time when he dared not leave his parish without permission from a magistrate ; when wages were practically fixed by these magistrates, who also administered the Poor

Law ; when he stood the chance of being har-
nessed to the parish cart, and the Commons
were being daily stolen from him by Acts
of Parliament passed by landowners only ;
when he might be imprisoned for collective
bargaining, or transported for snaring a
rabbit, or for being seen at night in a wood
or park in search of the fuel of which he had
been deprived by the Enclosure Acts. You
may tell him that his grandfather had
neither the vote nor free education ; that
wages were 8s. a week, and bread 1s. the
gallon loaf. Then, if you are a politician,
you will wisely recount to Hodge how he
has not only a vote, but also free education.
You will tell him of the Rural Magna Charta
of 1894, of the Housing and the Public Health
Acts, of the Small Holdings Acts, and, above
all, of the Old Age Pensions Act.

Then what will Hodge answer ? Probably
nothing at all. He has grown tired of can-
didates for Parliament, and he may keep
sullenly away from the Ballot Box, as the
Liberal Party found to its cost and its amazement at the last General Election. If he were
communicative he might answer something
like this—for as one who works with him
in the fields I may be allowed to express his
feelings in something like his own language :

" What you say may have been true enough

in my great-grandad's time, though when *I*
went to school our history book told us
nothing about these Enclosure Acts. It
seemed to jump right clean from the French
Revolution to the Battle of Waterloo, and
end there. Grandad did tell us as how the
poor were robbed of their land in our parish,
and that's how it is that no cottage folk now
can keep a cow nor any geese. I heard, too,
a man in one of those travelling vans tell of
it ; and how the House of Lords made a fuss
over the likes of us hiring land, though we
had to pay for it twice as dear as the farmer
pays for his. Yes, and how grandad did
nearly starve to death when bread was so
dear. Father has told us that, too. And
now we have what you call the Rural Magna
Charta, free education, and all those other
Acts you speak about. But are we any better
off than our *fathers*—not than our grand-
fathers ? That's how we look at it. Can
we get any more for our sovereign than they
did ? Do we stand up any bolder than they
did in front of the farmer or the squire ?
I am a married man with a family. I have
to pay, for nearly everything, more than what
my father did, and rents are going up more
than wages. Do you think I can leave my
parish any more than my great-grandfather ?
Well, I tell you straight, I can't. I have a

family to bring up on 15*s*. a week—some weeks I gets less, when regular wet weather sets in, or the land is frozen or snow-bound ; and if I keep my children well shod and their stomachs full, I gets behind with the tradesmen in the village, and we *can't* leave. Though sometimes our dinner is only potatoes, we never seems to have enough money saved to pay for moving even our few sticks. How am I better off, then ? You tell me that there are Housing Acts for us. To keep my children decent some of them ought now to have separate bedrooms, but do you think I am going to complain to my master, who lets me the cottage, or to the sanitary inspector ? Not I. I should only get turned out on to the roadside. Housing Acts don't put no roof over our heads. If my master heard me talking to you as I am now, I should soon have notice to quit—that is, just so soon as he could get someone else, perhaps a half gypo, or a lad, to take my place. You don't build any new cottages with your Acts—that's the trouble. You only closes them. What is the good of the Parish Council to us when all the power is left in the hands of the Rural District Councillors ? And who are they ? Why, the farmers who employ us. Even if we could afford to take a day off to serve once a fortnight, do you think we should get any work in the neighbourhood afterwards if we stood up against the likes of them ? Why, we are like Robin Hood—outlaws—that's what we are ; outlaws in our own country. The school officer comes to hunt up *our* children ; the sanitary inspector noses into *our* gardens, so that we can't keep a pig even. Your Public Health Act may be good, but it costs us money. When we want clean water to drink, it's another threepence a week ; and now there will be another three or four pence a week for insurance. Mr. Lloyd George means very well, I believe, but he don't understand what threepence or fourpence a week means when 15s. a week is not nearly enough to live upon. Mr. John Burns don't understand about housing in the country, that's certain, or he would not expect us to fill up forms we don't understand, and then ask us to make out a case. And he a working man, too ! Why, I'm told University men don't know how to fill up a Form they call Four. As to small holdings—well—I did apply for one, but I saw how annoyed my master was about it, and they were so long in finding the land that I drew back. I'm not sorry I did, as I haven't the money to work it. The Government don't seem to understand that taking a small holding is like taking a shop. You've got to stock it after you can see the rent. I say again that we ain't any better off, those of us who are poor. It comes every year harder to make both ends meet. But I tell you what this education *has* done: it has made the likes of us *less contented with our poverty than our fathers were.*"

It is true enough, I think, that nearly every " rural reform," with the exception of the Old Age Pension, has been costly to the agricultural labourer. The Enclosure Acts squeezed him out of his land. The Public Health Act has squeezed the pig out of his garden pigstye. The Town Planning Act has squeezed him out of 13,000 cottages, and found him only 116 new ones instead. Bacon Trusts, Cotton Syndicates, and Coal Combines have shorn him of food, fuel, and the shirt from his back.

It is always a difficult matter to make the prosperous English townsman realise the helplessness of Hodge. The foreigner, the German or Frenchman, coming from countries where the peasant is not a proletarian, grasps the situation far more readily when making a study of English rural life. In some respects the English country labourer of to-day is less able to stand up for his " rights " than was the French peasant before the French Revolution. This may sound an extreme statement ; but let me quote from J. L. Hammond's and Barbara Hammond's illuminating book, *The Village Labourer* :

> The French peasant may be overwhelmed by the dime, the taille, the corvée, the hundred-and-one services that knit his tenure to the caprices of a lord ; he may be wretched, brutal, ignorant, ill-clothed, ill-fed, ill-housed ; but he has not lost his status, he is not a casual figure in a drifting proletariat ; he belongs to a community that can withstand the lord, dispute his claims at law, resume his rights, recover his possessions, and establish one day his independence.

" *Ce seigneur litige avec ses vaisseaux,*" common enough then in France, cannot be written of the English peasant even a hundred and twenty years after the French Revolution ! Whoever heard of a country lawyer who would risk ruining his practice amongst the propertied class by championing the claims of a " drifting proletariat " ?

Possibly the most pitiful thing about the social life of rural England is the cowardice of the professional classes. Nor is it only the lawyer who exhibits a cowardice which many a town mechanic would scorn to show. Though the doctor knows perfectly well the insanitary conditions in which the labourers live, he remains discreetly silent. His children, like those of the parson, must go to a public school ; and how are the bills to be paid if a boycott of the possessing classes is instituted against him?

It took me and another man, who has now been made a J.P., exactly five years to have a National school made sanitary. Against us were ranged all the school managers, including the vicar, the drains of whose house ran into an open ditch under the windows of the school. Only one parent dared to come forward to give evidence as to the diphtheritic throats constantly recurring, and he was the coachman of my friend! Finally, it was only when the Board of Education threatened to close the school altogether, that the managers decided to put in a drain and fill up the ditch.

In spite, however, of the large number of parsons who side with the possessing class, and do so often quite unconsciously—it being a matter of tradition assimilated with the public school accent—there are others, and an increasing number I am glad to say, who realise that their Leader was a carpenter, and one who spent his life championing the poor and the oppressed. There is, for instance, the Rector of Tockenham, Wilts. And surely the very fact that he brought up two men from one village, who had given evidence at a Local Government Board Enquiry in the face of the opposition of the local farmers and of the agent of a great landowner, and two other labourers from another village who were prepared to give evidence—surely the fact that these men were shown before an audience in Caxton Hall in March 1912, as exceptionally brave men, is indicative that tyranny is rife in our countryside. And it is quite possible that the courage of two of these men, who had been evicted in a snowstorm, would not have had the necessary staying qualities, had they not been backed up by the National Land and Home League, of which Lord Henry Bentinck is the President.

The squire, or principal landowner, is often unnecessarily held in dread by the labourer; for the squire, with the increasing use of motors, is now often merely a bird of passage on his country estate. Most of his time, and that of the ladies of his household, is probably spent in a large town or abroad. England to him is a vast shooting-preserve, and he is not concerned as to whether Hodge sits on the Parish or the Rural District Council, though he may look askance at him should he ever meet him on the County Council. Hodge is too far off to trouble a squire whose business lies with the farmers; and in them the squire is little interested save as rent-payers and as tenants who will not bother him about the number of game kept in the woods. The tyranny of the squire over the labourer is not personal, like that of the farmer. The countryside must, of course, be kept open for birds, and the population kept in check, or sport might be ruined. The economic screw that the squire turns on the labourer is not to squeeze more rent out of his bones, as Cobbett would say, but to keep his class from swarming over the land.

On a recent motor tour into Suffolk, on which I was taken by a friend, it was appalling to notice the amount of land being badly farmed. Here and there between the huge partridge-drives, girdled by woods, lay forlorn villages, with an apologetic air, striving to efface their existence by decay. Some of the cottages bore the appearance of hulks, with their ribs lying exposed to wind and weather. The only sign of intensive culture discernible from Bishop's Stortford to Newmarket was on the dining-room table of the " Rutland Arms," where wheat was growing in pots as a cultural curiosity !

In one village—I may as well mention it : Great Bradley—I found the housing conditions, as a resident there declared, " worse than a London slum." The land is owned by a Peer of the Realm, and there is practically but one employer, and he a large farmer.

The Great Estate : One landlord, one farmer, and all the cottages farm-tied.   Great Bradley, Suffolk.

To face page 28.

With the farm are let a good many cottages
in the village. In one of these, two parents
and six children occupied the single bedroom
and the landing on the top of the stairs.
Rafters as bare as a bone and chimneys
tumbling down presented a tragic sight. An
old resident informed me that one poor street
in Upper Norwood was said to be peopled
by immigrants from Great Bradley. With
low wages, decaying cottages, and no land
for them to till free of thraldom, the young
had left as though a plague had devastated
the village. Two or three men had applied
for small holdings two years ago, but nothing
came of it. One of these had quickly to seek
work in the next parish after he had sent
in his application.

I am told that in a certain Suffolk parish,
when a labourer applied for a small holding,
a County Council officer confronted the
labourer with the one large farmer and asked
him to point out which of the farmer's fields
he would like !

Whilst political intimidation is sporadic,
breaking out acutely every five or six years,
the tyranny exercised by the farming class
over the labourer is an excoriation that knows
no rest. The large farmer is not only on the
Parish Council but is invariably to be found
on the Rural District Council, and very often

on the County Council. In the employer-landlord of the countryside are to be found the three jaws of Cerberus—the P.C., the R.D.C., and the C.C.—and he is the watch-dog to the domains of Pluto, who keeps the labourer imprisoned within the Hades of village life. His dog-in-the-manger policy, of preventing labourers from having access to the land, is one that is detrimental not only to the labourer but to all of us as Englishmen, for it leads to bad tillage. He is not concerned with making the land yield more when he adds field to field, but only with increasing his gross income and his control over the lives of others.

When I was elected on to a Parish Council in a certain Surrey village, it was only at night that I could visit the cottages of the poor in order to examine the water-supply, which was generally a stagnant pool. I did not wish to expose the tenants to the sight of the farmer-landlord when showing me the water that their children had to drink. Ranged against me on the Council were the three local farmers, their relatives, and their medical attendant. This group not only occupied all the farms in the parish, but also owned the local waterworks, the local gas-works, the mill, the butcher's shop, and most of the insanitary cottages. To this reigning

family of farmers the labourers had to come
for their daily work, their bread, their meat,
their drink, and their lodging. Their tyrannical domination over the village was almost
as complete as that portrayed by Balzac
when writing of the bourgeoisie in France
after the Revolution. The head of this
reigning family of farmers was chairman of
the Rural District Council, so that, should
anything pass a too progressive Parish Council,
it could be effectually blocked by the rural
House of Lords. Again, in the recent housing
scandal in Foxham, in Wiltshire, it was the
seven farmers against two labourers on the
Parish Council who declared, in the face of
impending evictions, that no cottages were
needed !

In some counties much hiring of labourers
is done by advertisement. " Good cottage
and garden " is the lure, and when Hodge,
with his family and household gods in the
cart, reaches the insanitary cottage, his bond-
age is complete. He cannot afford another
move, nor risk unemployment.

It is not only the man who has to suffer.
The territorial domination by one individual
sometimes strikes hard at those least able
to resist a blow. I know of one lady of the
Manor who has given orders to her steward
that no girl who " has got into trouble " shall

be allowed cottage-room on her estate. In these pages I have had to write of this in the form of fiction. I have called the story "A Pastoral of Hampshire." In quite a different county a pathetic appeal was made to me by a cowman who had been given notice to quit because his eldest unmarried daughter, aged nineteen, was enceinte. He had pleaded in vain to be allowed to remain, as his wife was about to give birth to another child. Needless to say the cottage was overcrowded.

If reform does not come quickly to re-people our empty countryside, either we shall lose our bold peasantry altogether, and with it our virility as a race, or a swift retribution will overtake the governing classes. "We steal the goose and give back the giblets," said a landowner to Thelwall, when commons were being enclosed. "No," came the retort, "giblets are much too dainty for the common herd, we give them only the pen feathers." It may be that a "drifting proletariat" will seize these pen feathers and with them write the laws by which rural England shall be governed.

CHAPTER II

THE ROMAN ROAD

The Roman Road runs straight and bare
As the pale parting-line in hair
Across the heath. And thoughtful men
Contrast its days of Now and Then,
And delve, and measure, and compare ;

Visioning on the vacant air
Helmed legionaries who proudly rear
The Eagle, as they pace again
The Roman Road.

THOMAS HARDY.

IT is curious to reflect that it was the great Roman Consul, Agricola, who laid the foundation of civilisation in Britain 1,800 years ago—Agricola, the husbandman. We can still foot the way where the Roman legionary marched, his armour flashing in the sunlight, nearly two thousand years ago, and note how we have continued the civilising work of Agricola, the husbandman, as we survey each side of the great Southern highway between Chichester and London.

Watling Street, the highway to the North,

3

was built on an old British trackway; but Stane Street, the Southern highway, is Roman to the core. It shares with the wall that runs from Solway Firth to the mouth of the Tyne the distinction of being one of the two great monuments that the Romans raised in this country.

Mr. Hilaire Belloc once said to the Sussex Archæological Society that the man who traces all the lost portions of the road from Regnum to Londinum will win immortal fame. I was not seeking fame when I tramped from Ockley, within the Surrey border, to Chichester. My interest was a living one.

It is not until you leave the North Downs behind you and feel yourself out of reach of those ever-spreading tentacles of that over-gorged octopus known as Greater London, and can look over your shoulders at Leith Hill, that you can begin to image Roman Britain.

At Ockley you can march for a mile or two along the undeflecting austerity of the Roman Road, but this is lost again amid a wild, luxuriant waste of vegetation, a tangle of woodland preserves for pheasants, and of rutty lanes, leading to isolated cottages amid ill-cultivated fields. For nearly three miles, during which I did not meet a solitary soul

working in the fields, the old road was over-
grown by brambles and underwood, and
cottages could be counted on the fingers of
one hand.

From Ockley to Roman Gate, you are, it
is true, off the beaten track of trade, but
there are nevertheless the open fields and the
woods, and though the time of the year—
mid-September—is between harvesting and
root-pulling, there was the work of scarifying
the stubble-fields, of ploughing, of manuring,
and sowing the winter corn to be done where
agriculture is seriously pursued as a craft.

Under the Romans, it should be remembered, agriculture prospered so well that
England soon became a corn-exporting country. The Saxons, from the time that they
ploughed, as the men of Sussex still do to-
day, with a team of bullocks, were good
agriculturists, as long as they were free men.
But the ploughshare and the sword are
hereditary foes, and when fighting became
common amongst them, with a big strong
man, or Thane, as overlord, the seeds of
feudalism were sown, and agriculture has
always thriven badly on that stony soil.

As you emerge from this tangled way at
Rowhook, you cross the high road immediately
and step out along the small portion of the
clearly defined Roman Way, mounting the

wooded crest before descending the delightful leaf-enveloped footpath through the hornbeam copse which brings you out to Roman Gate. The farther you go the more you realise how little we have attempted to people our own country opened up for us by the Romans. You pass a little schoolroom ; it is empty. There had been seven pupils at this National school erected for the village of Rowhook. It is now closed, and about a dozen children have to pick their way in all weathers through the drenching copse and patter along the exposed, open road, two and a half miles to Slindon, in order to learn a few scraps of the history of their country.

Those who like to travel at their ease should have a motor waiting for them at Roman Gate to whirl them along the straight, dusty, high road that strikes like a spear through the heart of Sussex, from Roman Gate to Pulborough. The country is tame ; the road is very straight and very long and, from the human point of view, very depressing. The absence of the field-worker might be anticipated through the wild and uninhabited and almost trackless part between Ockley and the Roman Gate ; but here you are once more on the king's highway, which has been in existence since Belinus, the Roman engineer, constructed it as a military road from Regnum to Londinum, giving his name to Billingshurst, and striking the strategic centre of Britain.

I was on foot save when I had a lift in a springless tumbril or a brewer's dray, and for the five miles along the highway into Billingshurst, between the hours of three and five, I saw only two men at work in the fields, and those were two old men spreading manure close to Slinfold village. Yet the road was flanked all the way by ordinary farm fields, few woods intervening.

The one thriving industry seems to be motoring. With the exception of the little hill at Pulborough, where the Romans were once encamped and from whence they took a wide survey of the surrounding country, there was nothing save police traps to prevent the motorist from running at top speed from the Roman Gate to the foot of the Downs. It is one of history's little ironies that on the road to Billingshurst I passed an Italian organ-grinder, grimacing for pence. Instead of the flash of steel, I met the obsequious bow.

I stayed at the " King's Arms," Billingshurst, for the night, setting out the next morning for Pulborough. This is a five-mile walk along a monotonously undeviating road, with meadows and stubble-fields on each side. On two farms only did I see men at work, until I got well within the parish of Pulborough. On the first of these a man (again an old man) was picking up stones in a field of mangolds. On the other farm, consisting of some five hundred acres, the two men at work were engaged in drawing water to bullocks in a field! One farmer I noticed had ventured a step from the cultural rucks of tradition. He had a crop of maize which would make excellent succulent food for cows in a season of drought. How slowly we move in agricultural science! The Saxons, for instance, quite understood the fertilising value of leguminous crops.

At Pulborough we enter a land of great estates of overlords, proud in the possession of vast pheasant-preserves, of parks large enough to contain cities—Petworth, Parham, Arundel, and Goodwood—and of unlimited hunting-ground. We begin to realise why colonisation has been stultified along the old Roman Road.

West Sussex stands pilloried among the four administrative counties, along with Derby, Westmoreland, and the West Riding of Yorkshire, for placing only 33 small owners on the land out of a population of 1,175,000. This is not surprising when one

thinks of the vast estates of the Dukes of
Arundel and Richmond, and of Earl Leconfield, within that great triangle of Down and
Weald land of which Petworth forms the
apex.   It has been said that Arundel is the
most feudal of all English towns.   Mr. E. V.
Lucas, that genial chronicler, has stated
that Arundel still depends for her life upon
the complaisance of her overlord.

" I know of no town with so low a pulse," he
writes, " as this precipitous little settlement under
the shadow of Rome and the Duke.   In spite of
picnicing parties in the Park, in spite of anglers
from London, in spite of the railway in the valley,
Arundel is still mediæval and curiously foreign.
On a very hot day as one climbs the hill to the
cathedral one might be in old France, and certainly
in the Middle Ages."

Mediæval as is Arundel, it is when we come
to the apex of this triangle—to Petworth—
that we realise to the full at how low a pulse
life can be lived even in the England of the
twentieth century.

Again I must quote Mr. E. V. Lucas.   I
must quote him because, in his *Highways and
Byways*, he writes for the tourist who walks
as an idler in the wilds and has no eyes for
social problems, for, rambling amid scenes of
placid beauty, he has no vision of physical
and spiritual decay.

" The town," writes Mr. E. V. Lucas, " seems to be beneath the shadow of its Lord even more than at Arundel ; it is like Pompeii with Vesuvius emitting glory far above. One must of course live under the same conditions if one is to feel the authentic thrill ; a mere sojourner cannot know it. One wonders in these feudal towns what it would be like to leave democratic London, or the independence of one's country fastness, and pass for a while beneath the spell of a Duke of Norfolk, or a Baron Leconfield—a spell possibly not cast by them at all but existing none the less, largely through the fostering care of the townspeople on the rent roll, largely through the officer controlling the estates ; at any rate unmistakable, as present in the very air of the streets as is the presage of a thunderstorm. Surely, to be so dominated, without actual influence, must be very restful. Petworth must be the very home of low-pulsed peace ; and yet a little oppressive too, with the great house and its traditions at the top of the town—like a weight on the forehead. I should not like to make Petworth my home, but as a place of pilgrimage, and a stronghold of architectural taste, it is almost unique."

Mr. Lucas writes like a literary artist ; and one suspects that even as a chronicler of Highways and Byways he has a glimmering of something lurking within the rose-covered porch of the labourer's cottage, something behind the tradesman's door that would make a pretty tragedy if it were ever dragged to light.

In the time of the Confessor this manor

was worth £118. A few years later it was only worth the price of a stall at a theatre. I wonder how many thousands of pounds it is worth now !

From the minatory coign of vantage such as Pulborough Hill one's mind instinctively takes flight back through the centuries and visualises

> The Roman watch-fires glow
> Red on the dusk ; and harsh
> Cries a heron flitting slow
> Over the valley marsh
> Where the sea-mist gathers low.

We wonder, as we dream over a waste almost empty of life, how much we have really built a road to freedom ; whether we have really ever opened the gateway to civilisation. Here we have still the husks of feudalism grasped tightly by those to whom they were thrown by a prodigal monarch. The spirit of it, too, is unfortunately not yet dead. Across the marshes are to be seen the offensive new turrets of Amberley Castle.

Three years ago I raised a protest in one of the daily papers against the threatened exclusion of the public from the old castle grounds by the erection of some newly painted boards, put up over the public entrance, worded " These Grounds are Private." At the same time Mr. Edward Stott, A.R.A.

(who lives at Amberley), from an archæological interest worded a plaint to the Duke of Norfolk—the owner of the castle—against the tearing down of the ivy from the old walls and the erection of huge scaffolding set up for the apparent purpose of restoring the castle. Representation was made to the Rural District Council to intervene in the interest of the public as to right of way. But the Council were all more or less Duke's men, and how could a farmer with probably only an annual tenancy afford to offend the Estate Office ! Though seriously threatened in this manner, the public right through the castle has never been denied. But inconceivable as it seems in one who is the premier peer of the realm and the owner of another large castle—Arundel—the restoration was proceeded with, and when I turned aside from the Roman Road I saw the finishing touches being put to two castellated turrets which guard the bridge over the moat. One does not object to an old castle being used as a farmstead, or to seeing a twentieth-century cream-separator worked on fourteenth-century masonry, but this futile rebuilding is the kind of thing you expect at the hands of an American millionaire inflated with the lust of numbering an antique castle amongst his many possessions.

A pair of inhabited cottages on the Duke of Norfolk's estate. Rain comes through the tiled roof and beats through the walls. The windows can only be opened at the risk of the panes dropping out.

To face page 42.

The extent to which this fertile Weald has
been denuded of life strikes us with tragic
insistence as we pass Hardham along the old
Road. Hardham once boasted of a monastic
institution, and around it we can envisage at
one time a thriving population. Now, a
dreary little church is all that is left of it,
a church measuring roughly fifty feet by
twenty-one feet, with three slits for windows
in the wall facing the road. Rural industries
seem to be represented by three gipsies engaged
in making rabbit-nets on a piece of roadside
waste.

I was bent now on making my way as
quickly as I could, excited at the thought of
entering the low gateway of a hut which
ushers us into the basement of the home of
an ancient and splendid civilisation.

It was exactly a hundred years ago that
Mr. Tupper's great-grandfather discovered
this romantic flooring of a Roman villa. The
ploughshare, which will probably outlast the
sword, first laid bare to us these precious
stones.

Nothing in all England reveals to us the
Roman occupation so dramatically as the
swinging open of this door of a thatched
shed. We step at once from the twentieth
back into the second century.

And it is not the wonderfully preserved

inlaid figure of Ganymedes, nor the head of Juno, nor that of Winter, nor the fixed and lasting stare of Medusa, nor the remains of the hot-water pipes for heating the rooms, that bring the Romans so intimately near to us ; it is the footprint of a dog and a sandal-shod Roman who had ventured on to the clay tiles whilst still wet and left their impress for all time.

It was pleasant, when one emerged as it were from a world of ancestral shadows, to find oneself treading a footpath across a sun-lit field of mangolds. Gazing round at this thriving farm, one felt that this land could grow something if it were only given a chance. In one stubble-field I counted six ploughs at work. Here was English farming at its best. A woman who lodged me one night under her reed-thatched roof at the foot of the South Downs remarked that the land seemed to "have got into too big lumps." You are soon made aware of this as you climb those great sweeping landmarks of southern England, the South Downs, and light upon the boundary stones dividing one estate from another. In this rough-and-ready way are the South Downs—*our* South Downs—carved out into great chunks between a Lord Zouche on the one side and a Duke of Norfolk on the other.

The notice board over the right of way through Amberley Castle.

To face page 44.

Unless you have better luck than I did you will meet no one to ask the way across the Downs, for I did not see a soul the two miles I was climbing, save a shepherd in the far distance herding a flock of South-downs, their bells tinkling like running water singing down a wooded dell. On leaving the Roman villa, cultivated land seemed to have been left behind for good. No more were visible those strips of tilled land that on the northern slope are shaped like flint arrow-heads, striking into the heart of the Downs.

Close to the Roman Way on one of these strips, where rape was being grown for sheep, I found an old labourer bending manfully to his work with the hoe, still pursuing the life of toil that he had begun at the tender age of seven.

Near him, in the centre of the field, he had placed his coat with his lunch under an umbrella. This little black pile of personal effects impressed itself upon me, showing as it did in what isolation worked the field labourer of the South Downs. His first job, he told me, when he was seven years old, was, with stick in hand, to prevent the bullocks from crossing the dry dykes on the marshes. By eight he was out ploughing with his father in the fields, but so small was he that a hop-

pole had to be fixed to the plough to prevent
the horses from treading him down with
their great hoofs, as he turned their heads
at the end of a furrow. He supposed he
would go on working, turning over the soil
which had nourished him so poorly, until the
time came when someone would throw a
spade of Downland earth over his toil-
smitten body. No note of discontent passed
from his lips. He had endured so long that
it was not worth while to worry with problems at his time of life. And *this* after
Agricola, the husbandman, had civilised
Britain nearly two thousand years ago!

Stretching before you on the top of the
Down is a rolling expanse of beech woods
which extend southwards like green foam,
and far beyond lies the glittering sea. This
is a wonderful wood, this North Wood, and
yet a young gamekeeper employed by Lord
Leconfield told me that few ever visited it.
There is a magic light in the green depths
of this embowered Roman roadway. The
western sun fills it with an entrancing beauty,
lighting up the clean beech-boles like altar
fires. Above, their delicate leaves catch with
fairy hand the burning light, but to transmute
it into ether, green and cool, in which it is
exquisite to bathe your hot and tired limbs.

The great industry here is shooting, and

The old Roman road. Notice the padlock on the gatepost.

To face page 47.

woe betide the village child who walks up from
Eartham or Slinfold to gather blackberries or
any of the other wild fruits of the earth which
ripen but to rot amid the luxuriant brambles.

Enter these enchanted woods,
You who dare!

In the heart of it I met a woodman. I
fancied I had wandered off the track, and
I asked him the way. Unlike the usual docile,
sluggish men of Sussex, his eyes blazed with
revolt.

"You'll find a gate with a padlock and
chain across the old Roman Road," he said.
"Here, wait a minute!" he called out,
seeing me about to move on. He took a
clasp-knife out of his pocket. "Look'ee,"
he cried as he stepped aside to a beech tree,
"I give ten shillings for this tree"; and with
his knife he marked a cross on its bark.
"And for this one, see, I might give a pound.
Well, and they git all the underwood and
all the shootin', and it costs them nuthin',
and yet they do grumble about a ha'penny
in the pound—a ha'penny in the pound!
My wife, and your wife, mind you, are not
allowed to enjoy it. And they even putt a
padlock to the geate acrost the old Road—
ourn road—but they can't shet it up, I tell
you, they can't do it."

His chuckle resounded in the depths of the wood long after I had left him. I recalled it when I saw that the padlock and the chain were around the gate-post only—the gate itself was wide open !

Here you cross the highroad leading to Eartham and enter a gate nearly opposite where there is a right-of-way along the old Road which has been challenged by some modern landowner. You pursue the bridle-way to Seabeach, no doubt so called because the flints here were drawn all the way from Selsey Bill. You come now into the heart of the Duke of Richmond's property, a fact of which you are soon apprised, for at Halnaker miles of wall intimate that the modern rendering of the old text is, " The earth is the landlord's, and the fulness thereof."

Close by is Boxgrove Common. It was once, no doubt, the common property of those that settled round the old priory. Now apples hang in the pageantry of autumnal colour over the green graves of those English who once held this land in common possession. The Common is now fenced in and has become part of the Duke of Richmond's many thousand acres. Above the park, on the Downs, lies a stretch of land that could feed many flocks of sheep, yet few were to be seen grazing on that great green pasturage.

It was in the calm of a Sabbath evening that I entered Halnaker to seek a bed. The village street looked friendly enough with its lighted windows under tall, dark elms, while here and there water in the cart-ruts held their reflected light like jewels. I had been walking for four miles between the hours of 5 and 7, and I had not met a single soul. I had some trouble to find anyone who was able to let me a bedroom. The village inn could not give me shelter, and it is a sinister reflection that, though we are now so highly civilised, even on a great Southern highway there are few cottages built with more than two bedrooms.

It is fitting that the Roman Road should end—or begin, as you will—in a cathedral city, the core of country life, the apogee of English civilisation ; and yet by the time I had ended my pilgrimage at the Cross I had met more poverty in the streets of Chichester than in the whole of my walk.

One's imagination visualises the Roman warrior, erect and efficient, in glittering armour, proudly marching out of Regnum to conquer and to civilise. And then one recoils at the thought of the grimacing organ-grinder on the road to Billingshurst ; recoils at the thought of the man at seventy-one still hoeing rape ; and recoils still more at the

4

stunted, crushed, woe-begone citizens that loaf about the narrow, overcrowded streets of Cissa's Ceastre, all members of an Imperial race. London, like Chichester at the other end of the Roman Road, is overcrowded with ill-clad, ill-nourished beings, and between the two lie the silent Downs with many a beautiful, sheltering slope empty of life, and the vast, open Weald with land starving for the fructifying touch of labour.

We await some bold constructive policy of colonisation such as a modern Agricola might have projected. Shall we perchance have to wait until a son of the people, some intellectual shepherd of the Downs, with clarified vision, arises to re-colonise the lonely land through which the Roman Road still passes with enduring, undeviating austerity, and so continue that work of civilisation the foundation of which was laid nearly two thousand years ago?

CHAPTER III

1. *A Pastoral of the Downs*

A CHARMING downland village, with a wide expanse of the blue sea visioned from the top of the serene Downs ; a downland village, devoid of any outward sign of poverty, of low wages and bad housing. Here the motorist or the superficial tourist, with eyes alone for external beauty, would be amazed should you tell him that the people were living in a state of villainage under the rule of one or more tyrants, to whom they were beholden for their bread and butter as well as for the roof over their heads.

The rector was unhappy. Like most country parsons well on in years, he sought peace in his village; for though of a military bearing, and one who had supplied sons for the British army, he sought not the rôle of the angel with the flaming sword. He loved his books ; but greater than the love of his books was his love for his garden, in which

51

a tennis court of fine downland turf was an attractive feature to his two dozen grand-children who came to stay with him from time to time.

" This notoriety is all very painful to me," he said. " I would not have opened my lips at all at the Rural Housing Conference, but that Lord Strachie asked me to speak. Already Mr. ——'s bailiff, who is my church-warden, has complained to me that I need not have made all this fuss now that every-thing was getting on so nicely in our village."

(It is an extraordinary thing that country vicars, even democratic vicars, should in-variably choose for their churchwarden men of this type.)

The rector's statement, which had electri-fied so many good people as it went the round of the London papers, was that housing con-ditions were so bad in his own district that he had known of a girl of fourteen who slept in a chest of drawers in an overcrowded cottage, and of four lodgers in a single room who had endured these housing conditions until the middle of their room was occupied by a fifth lodger !

Great landowners have many ways of punishing vicars who zealously try to apply to daily life the ethics of the Sermon on the Mount. One was mean enough to keep back paying his tithes beyond even the legal time limit. Fortunately, the rector had private means, for had he been circumstanced like a neighbouring vicar who is " passing rich on eighty pounds a year," and been obliged to tell the butcher not to call for at least three months, things might have gone hard with him in this Christian land of ours.

"The people will not speak to *you*, a stranger, of their troubles," said the rector to me. " They will not tell you if they are overcrowded or underpaid."

The Sussex man is indeed very reticent concerning the vital facts of his existence. Should you stay at the inn and listen to the conversation in the taproom, you would glean nothing that would enlighten you as to the tragedy of his daily life. As his hands grasp the pewter pot, the shadows which dogged his footsteps to the door of the inn creep away. The romance of life lies behind those brightly lit red blinds. And this is the kind of conversation you would hear.

" I'll lay yer don't clear one ditch."

" Who said I was a-goin' to clear it ? "

" Not if you run as yer did tother day, I'll lay a pint as yer don't."

" I knowed a man from Ringmer——"

" Yes, old Jimmy had a good innings—

72, and hisn was the hunderth grave I duggen in my time."

" It's when you git among them jockeys in the South of France——"

" I say, I knowed a man from Ringmer——"

" If I ketch you up my apple tree, I'll——"

" Well, a man walked into my shallot bed, a man you wudna' have thought, neither."

" Any man what takes what isn't 'isn, wants a tidy good clump on the side of the head."

" Well, I reckon everyone did ought ter 'ad a clump some time in his lifetime."

" You speak for yoursel'."

" I be."

" Are you workin' for old —— (squire) ? "

" No damned fear."

" I knowed a man from Ringmer who——"

" I picked up that lamb at the foot of the hill beyond that yaller kilt. The yoe couldn't give him a drop—I carried him home and suckled him. Now he's as fat as a mole."

" I knowed a man from Ringmer who——"

I never got to hear what the man from Ringmer did, for it was closing time when the speaker was querulously making another attempt to be heard, and you would probably not hear one word of revolt in this village

symposium, carried on through the whole
evening in the taproom of the inn.   But outside, in the dark, unlighted street, under the
stars, if you gain his confidence, perhaps
the Sussex labourer will speak to you as man
to man.

Only then will you learn of the shadows
that lie across the threshold of every home.
You will hear how the whole village is ruled
by one man, or rather by two men.   One
represents the *nouveaux riches* ; the other,
the old landed aristocracy, with a son to
protect his landed interests sitting in the
House of Commons.   The first has won his
way to riches through keeping a safe seat
on a fast horse, and now conducts a racing
stable.   To him belongs most of the village
and immediate farm-lands : the other lays
claim to a great stretch of the Downs, where
sheep may live but where men decay.

No revolutionary note is sounded by these
patient, docile men—not even under the stars
at night.   They do not expect the land to
belong to them although they are English,
nor the cottages either, for they are men of
Sussex and content with things as they are,
if only they get what they call fair treatment.
Their wages are only 14s. a week.   An occa-
sional good shepherd may get 17s., with
perhaps £2 as lambing money.   Out of this

3s. 6d. has generally to be paid away in rent.
Low wages and the payment of rent are to
them as inevitable as death. They take
them as a matter of course. What really
hurts these men—hurts their sense of human
dignity—is the treatment meted out to them
by the lords of the soil, and there is no one
but the old rector to help them, to bring a
breath of freedom into their lives. They
are lucky indeed to have a rector of the
Church Militant on their side.

Their allotments have just been taken away
from them, because the purchaser of the land
on which were tilled these field-gardens
had declared his intention to convert them
into his kitchen garden. The villagers did
not ask for small holdings, they did not ask
for allotments in the sense that many
Parish Councils attach to allotments—that
is, many acres given over to field-gardens.
The total amount of land for which they
asked amounted to one and a half acres.
One and a half acres for a whole village of
labourers !

The successful jockey-landowner had stated
that he could not spare any land, in spite of
the fact that many of his fields were, as
I passed through them, crimson with poppies
and golden with charlock.

On the other side of the village the owner

gave a curt refusal to grant even a rood of
land ; a refusal which is incomprehensible,
unless it be that he fears men might become
riotously independent by tilling, at a high
rent, a few roods of land.

The village has no Parish Council, only a
Parish Meeting, and no one, apparently, takes
the initiative; no independent gentleman, Nonconformist minister, or schoolmaster ; no one,
save the rector.

" Why don't you demand land from the
County Council," I asked a labourer outside
the village inn when the lights were extin-
guished, " by sending in your names together ? "

" That's more than our place be worth—
we should lose our homes too," he answered.

" But there are Acts of Parliament now,"
I said to him, " passed so that you can get
land and cottages without going before the
squire at all."

" What's the good of them for the likes of
us ? Why it's more than we durst; for if
any one of us spoke up or signed a paper,
we should lose our place and our home, too,
I tell ye."

Then it was, in the dark village street,
shadowed by elms, and with no landlord or
farmers within hearing, that I learnt how the
head shepherd of an estate was told by the

bailiff to find room in his cottage for six stable lads. There were only three bed-rooms in his cottage, which were already fully occupied by the shepherd, his wife, and six children, one of whom was a girl of eighteen. Although the shepherd dared not refuse his landlord-employer, I am glad to say this villainous order was never carried out—the local sanitary authorities inter-posed in time.

There is another cottage in this village which has only one bedroom : in this slept a man and his wife, an anæmic-looking daughter of sixteen, and another of twelve. In the last fifteen years only two cottages had been built, and these two were let at 5s. a week each, a price out of the reach of the agricultural labourer.

Close by is a group of four cottages to which until quite recently there was only one E.C. To a group of cottages in the village street not a single piece of guttering has been fixed to catch rain-water, which is valuable in a village where one public well has to serve about twenty cottages ; and when it rains, the denizens of these cottages rush out with baths and pails and basins to catch the precious liquid and with infinite trouble store it for use. How often do we hear the complaint, " Why can't the poor keep them-

selves clean? It costs nothing to be clean."
It costs a great deal. The effort is herculean,
where every drop has to be fetched in a pail.
Close by are some waterworks, but no landlord, no public authority attempts to cleanse
these Augean stables of the poor.

The village is surrounded by thousands of
acres of health-giving Downland, where for
many a mile not a spiracle of blue smoke
from a cottage chimney is to be seen : only
the beckoning black trail of smoke-emitting
liners taking emigrants to a happier land.
There is ample space here under God's
heaven for men to live peaceably together
without jostling and stifling one another,
but neither of the lords of the soil will
yield a yard of even sheep-grazing land to
house the makers of England. Acts of
Parliament are of little avail if the people
for whom they are passed are afraid to move
hand or foot and step across the village street
to put them into force.

In the same village are stables in which
horses are housed in luxury, even with
splendour. To record the words of the good
old rector, " the horses are housed like princes
and the peasants like pigs."

A four-mile walk across the Downs without
passing a single cottage brings us to another
beautiful Downland village where racing is

again "the chief industry." It is a walk bracing enough to evoke from us a shout of thanks that we live in southern England, where westward ridge upon ridge of Down meets the eye, and to the south the olive green of the Downs is merged in the blue of the sea. It is an open bown country, as Cobbett would call it, where the air is like wine, and shadowless save when a racing cloud passes over the sun and spills, like a swift sower, over the hill and down into the dale, a shadowy balloon bag of soot over the darkened herbage.

One should give thanks, I say, were one not haunted by the thought that this empty countryside (across which I met but one man, and he a shepherd), lying locked in the hands of one or two great owners, means a life of toil, tyranny, and destitution to those who live behind the cottage doors.

"This village could grow," said the country doctor to me, " if——"

" If it were not throttled by those who hold the land around it," I added.

He nodded acquiescence.

But Government is busy always with expansion abroad, and rarely thinks of expansion at home, where our population is either too sparsely scattered or too closely herded together.

Here we have again beauty enshrined within an old-world atmosphere. Tourists travel all the way from New England to revel in the village homes of old England, and writers and painters become enthusiastic over the magnetic, external charm of the place. Probably there is no other district so typical of old-world Saxon rural England. But what does the labourer think about its charm, who has to bear the heat and burden of the day on 14s. a week, and with this money has to purchase food, clothing, boots, house-room, and insurance against sickness for himself, wife, and family: a sum which the gay tourist would expend on himself in a day at the old inn of the district ?

Though no one, to my knowledge, has spoken of it, no publicist has written of it, no M.P. has ever raised his voice in indignation over it (for have not these simple men of Sussex chosen a Sussex man to represent them !), the price the labourer has to pay to inhabit a cottage is scandalous.

Rack-renting is as rife here for cottagers as it has ever been for Irish peasants. Under a certain landlord a shepherd, who had just been promoted to the crook on 15s. a week for seven days' labour, told me that he and his brother paid 7s. 6d. a week for their cottage. This I could hardly believe until I came to talk with a labourer's wife in a neighbouring hamlet. She pointed out to me two cottages remaining empty which the squire was trying to let for 7s. 6d. and 4s. 6d. respectively, though other landlords are letting their cottages at from 2s. to 3s. 6d. a week. They were old labourers' cottages, of four rooms only, with the addition in the case of the 7s. 6d. one of a pantry—that is, of an extra cupboard. Such a rack-rent could, of course, be only squeezed out of the bones of a labourer, or out of those of his wife and little children.

"*He's* a terror," said the woman—"*he* don't want no one to live but hisself. No one will work for him unless they can't find no other job. My two sons won't. One works for Mr. H——. He is a fair man. He do pay 3d. an hour for any overtime. (Think what is left unsaid by this statement!) But the squire! Do you know our minister's wife told me that a poor widow woman one day went gathering blackberries on his side of the hedge. She only did it because she wanted to earn a little money to buy some boots for her children to go to school in in wet weather—and when he saw her with her can of blackberries he went and spilled them all out on to the ground."

A flush of righteous indignation spread over the woman's face. "Why," she said,

" if I'd been there I'd have smacked his face ! "

" Is he as mean as that ? " I asked.

" As mean as that ! " she said. " You ask farmer if he dares shoot a rabbit on his farm."

" But the farmer is protected by the Ground Game Act."

" *That* don't matter. He would be told to go if he did."

Here the woman expressed the countryman's firm conviction that Acts of Parliament avail nothing against tyrants who hold the means of livelihood in their hands. This is the kind of tyranny that endures in rural England. It is, as I have said, not political, but the omnipresent economic intimidation, that is harder to be endured. Probably these cottage folk held the same political opinions as the tyrant who oppressed them.

On a large estate adjoining it has been the custom of an owner who has been noted for his fairness to keep the letting of the cottages in his own hands, the cottagers paying their rent quarterly to him instead of to the farmer who employed them. Now, unfortunately, through his death, the agents have been allowed to let the cottages with the farms, presumably because it saves trouble in rent-collecting, and the labourers are left in a more deplorably dependent position than they were a generation ago.

Even shepherds seem to have declined from their status on these farms, and it is a bitter reflection that probably they are not any better off now on 15s. a week than they were on 9s. a week in the days of the Hungry Forties. An old shepherd, with whom I talked whilst he was training a young sheep-dog with a flock of lambs, seemed to walk in fear of the eye of the farmer. With infinite patience, although the scorching mid-summer's sun was striking down upon his battered old hat, he would single out a lamb with his crook, capsize it, lay it on its back between his legs, and crying, " The fly do terrify the poor dears," he would immediately dress the afflicted parts with ointment. I offered him a piece of tobacco, with which he filled his pipe, but catching sight of the straw hat of the farmer coming across the adjoining field of clover, he remarked with resignation, " I'll wait till he goes before I lights up."

One wonders, as the outline of the Long Man carved on the great slope of Wilmington Hill arrests the eye, whether the " free " English village labourer of to-day is any better off materially than the Saxon churl ploughing his "yard" of land furrow-long with his team of

oxen owned by the village community. The
Saxon was sure of his strip of land, at any rate
—a strip as long as the oxen could draw the
plough without stopping to rest, while the
landless English labourer of the twentieth
century finds it difficult to gain his allotment
of a few rods.

Over the crown of the Long Man is now
driven into the turf, by some vandal owner,
a great white post with a notice-board. At
his feet another post is driven into the
Down turf. This figure, with his long staffs,
pierced at the crown and at the feet by great
white nails, is symbolical of the Good Shepherd
crucified by the lords of the soil probably at
the very time when this great figure was
limned on the hillside. On the great spacious
Downs there are but few resting-places for
the soles of the feet of those sons of men who
toil with their hands.

2. *A Pastoral of the Cotswolds*

A ruined cottage, gaping open to every wind
of the Wold, stood on one side of the road.
A branch of an apple tree thrust an exquisite
spray of pink-and-white petals into a dis-
mantled bedroom. Against the one sound
wall of the cottage stood intact a shed, from
which emerged hens. Cattle, too, found

5

shelter there at night with a sound roof over their heads, for cattle assuredly are of more importance than human beings. A labourer can be replaced any day without financial loss ; a cow cannot.

On the other side of the road my attention was arrested by the tocsin sounded by a swarm of wild bees issuing from a hole in an old hedgerow elm. Over the hedge a toil-smitten woman, sun-bonneted, was weeding the winter-sown wheat. I pointed to the swarm of bees and the reward awaiting a courageous arm. But she shook her head. Then I pointed to the demolished cottage, and asked her if there were many like this one in her part of the country.

" If you go down to our village," she said, " you will find many like that. I can re-member thirty cottages tumbling down in my time."

" And have no new ones been built ? "

" Ne'er a one," she answered laconically. At the sound of horse's footsteps she hastily bent her back again to her work. An old man on a well-groomed horse rode up. He had small, sharp eyes and a thin, long upper lip.

" It's this sort of thing," I said, pointing to the broken-down cottage, " that makes cycling amongst the Cotswolds more wearisome than mounting the long sweep of the curved hills."

"It don't pay to build," came the quick retort.

I remarked meditatively, "I suppose not, with wages at twelve shillings a week."

"It's the state of the country," he answered, in a tone as though he had bitten a crab apple ; "that's what it is. Wages are higher than they have ever been, and yet we get less skilled labour. I farm a thousand acres, so I ought to know. Would you believe it, the other evening I found one of my farm lads doing a sum at the night-school that *I* couldn't do ? But do you think I can trust him to do anything on the land ? Not a bit of it. And I suppose he'll be off to a town job soon. It's this education that has done the mischief."

"Insufficient education of the right kind, of course you mean," I responded. "But if they had the chance to work some land for themselves, perhaps they would stay. They might then earn sufficient to pay the rent of a decent house."

"A small holding ? What's the good of them ? Look at Fels."

"But I could have told you that Mr. Fels's holdings were doomed to failure three years ago. Nevertheless, there are thousands of men who have made a success of their small holdings in Worcestershire, Lincolnshire—and even in Essex."

He quickly changed the subject, and noticing my camera, suggested that I should photograph the church of which he was a warden. He also invited me to look at the old Manor House where he and his forbears had lived for over a hundred years.

The signpost pointed towards his retreating figure. It indicated Great Risington— *Great* Risington, mark you. His retreating figure, too, was indicative of Great Risington.

I had come six miles from Stow-on-the-Wold. Half a mile down the hill I entered the village. Here the tragedy of rural England stood unmasked without even the glamour of the picturesque. Three cottages behind the village inn looked as though the army of some conquering foreigner had invaded the Cotswold Hills and riddled the cottages with holes. A turn to the right, up the lane, stood the ruins of a group of cottages. Down the village, towards the church, in a group of three cottages it was patent how the canker of decay was eating into village life. The first cottage had been reduced to a skeleton. It showed only its lean walls, with the rafters stripped of every thread of thatch. The cottage joining

The roof is off the end cottage, the next is boarded up and uninhabited, whilst the nearest one is already doomed. The entire village of Great Rissington is tumbling down in this manner.

To face page 68.

it had the shutters up. It was closed as uninhabitable. The third was still inhabited, but the canker of decay was sure to reach it in the course of a brief year or two. On the other side of the road one could read the same dreary story.

As I was photographing these remnants of an English peasant life the rector came upon me.

"Twenty cottages have tumbled down since I became rector, sixteen years ago," he informed me with wrinkled brows.

He was a little disturbed when I told him that I meant to write about and perhaps publish these poignant pictures of a deserted village.

"But what can we do?" he asked. "The rent is only 1s. 6d. a week, and the squire is a poor man, although he does own three villages. Lloyd George has robbed him of all his superfluous cash."

The Budget, I reminded him, became law only in 1909, and as he could remember cottages tumbling down for many years, during which time no attempts had been made to rebuild, his statement seemed to me an odd one.

"Still," I said, "why trouble the squire? Why not stir up the public authorities?"

The rector sighed ; said it was all regrettable

but inevitable, and opening a book, bound in vellum, which treated of dead things, turned away without offering any hope of a solution. I felt sorry I had disturbed him ; he had greeted me with such a smiling face.

A village tradesman here spoke to me bitterly of the decline in the population. "There is no chance for a man here," he said. "The farmers don't keep a sheep to the acre, and but one labourer to the hundred acres. There is a five-hundred-acre farm here where only a shepherd, a cowman, a ploughman, and one field-labourer are kept. But they won't let anyone else have a try. There's some charity land near here that's been growing nothing until a labouring man began to till it."

I next accosted a labourer in the village. He told me that his wages did not average 12s. a week, taking into account the wet days, and that his children had to live chiefly upon bread and lard and potatoes. Labourers, he said, were afraid to apply for land or new cottages. He, too, complained that the large farmers, who grudged giving up a rood of land, barely kept a sheep to the acre and one man to every hundred acres. Only small stock holdings would be of any use there to the working man, and he had no capital wherewith to start one. He knew of only one labourer who had obtained land, and he had made a success of farming it.

My acquaintance on horseback now came out of the old Manor House to invite me within. The labourer, casting a quick glance at him, turned hurriedly away.

He carried a long-handled axe over his shoulder, and in spite of this formidable weapon being firmly gripped by a sinewy hand, he spoke with timidity and in a low voice when I asked him about the conditions of village life. He was young and sturdy, this son of the soil, and he struck me as one who would make a splendid sapper. Instead, he was a crestfallen hewer of wood. He walked away with a lopping, lifeless stride. It seemed strange to think that he was one of an Imperial race. No pride of race was visible in his dejected carriage.

" I learn," I said to him who rules this immediate countryside (he was the vicar's churchwarden and the squire's agent, probably he was also Chairman of the Parish Council and a member of the Rural District Council—but of this I am not sure), " that you have one man here who has a small holding, and that he is doing fairly well."

" Ah, yes, there now," said the old gentleman, his face brightening, " that man came to me fifteen years ago, when he was only

earning 11s. a week, and asked me if I would
sell him a cow. Then he had only the use
of his cottage garden, where he kept a sow and
some poultry. I told him I would sell him an
old cow for £8, but I asked him if he knew
what a big job he was undertaking, for,
besides the cow he would want a churn, a
pail, a crock, and pan. And then what
about land ? He said he could rent a grass
field from the rector. The next day he
came with the eight sovereigns in the one
hand, and a halter in the other. He bought
a few dairy utensils from me, and that, I
believe, was the whole of his capital, with the
pig and the hens. Now, to-day, he farms
eighty acres, on which he keeps no fewer than
forty head of horned cattle and four horses,
and by taking his butter into market every
week he has established a carrier's business.
But then, mark you, he was the right sort.
He wasn't like *some*. He kept outside the
public house. . . . Will you have a drop of
whisky ? "

" And how much rent does he pay ?

" Some fields 15s. an acre, others £1, and I
know he pays £2 for a good bit of grazing land.
Let me see : he has five different landlords."

" His land lies in various parts of the
parish, he has to go many miles to market
his produce, and yet you say he makes his

small holding pay ! Why, you must believe in small holdings even more than I do."

" Ah, but he was the right sort, you know," my host answered ruefully.

" So are most men when given the opportunity," I remarked. Surely, I thought, unless something is done, and done quickly, by the Government to speed up the creaking administrative machinery of Housing Acts or establish a minimum wage, this village, like many others about here, will be denuded of human life.

I was cycling to Little Barrington, where a Cirencester lady wrote to me that the decay of village life was so woeful to look upon that it had broken her heart. But I never reached Little Barrington. There was quite enough matter to arrest my attention at Great Risington. I returned to Stow-on-the-Wold. Perhaps some other writer will some day journey to Little Barrington and write of its perishing life. " There are," wrote my correspondent, " eight or nine cottages all in a row, empty ; and yet thousands of acres are lying idle and scores of fine youths emigrating to Canada."

Stow-on-the-Wold is a little country town left high and dry amid the Cotswolds, stranded almost entirely from the track of trade. There certainly is a railway station, but it lies in the valley a mile and a half away. Stow-on-the-Wold itself stands serene, grey-stoned, and steeped in a mediæval atmosphere.

If you feel so disposed you can come here and experience the authentic thrill of a past age. That is to say, if you be one of the booted and spurred, and able to enjoy the luxury of being an idler in the wilds. That seems to be the spirit in which most people take up their quarters in villages old enough to bear a market cross. I do not complain of this village. It is perhaps better than those ravaged by bustling, commercial enterprise. But there is here that diffidence displayed by those who can afford to live sequestered lives in beautiful places, which keeps them from delving deep down into the lives of those whose cottages are smothered with honeysuckle and briars.

It is the old story here. It is the story the source of which you can trace to every village where labourers have been denied access to the land, and where the administrative councils are composed of those who toil not, neither do they spin. And yet little country towns like Stow-on-the-Wold, which can boast of an Urban District Council, cannot sink into the same Slough of Despond in which villages like Great Risington stagnate. In Great Risington, and in hun-

dreds of other villages like it, there is absolutely no one, if the parson takes no action,
to fight for a life of greater freedom for
the village labourer. That is the pitiful
tragedy of these villages.

Isolated from their fellows, rarely seeing
a paper which writes of a larger outlook on
life, and only coming into contact with that
larger outlook when someone returns from
Canada to tell them about a country where
a man is treated as a man and not as someone's servant, these village labourers of the
Cotswolds lead lives entirely cut off from the
stream of modern movements ; there is no one
to take the initiative in such villages—no
one that in any sense represents the labourer.

In larger villages which have risen to the
pride of townships, like Stow-on-the-Wold,
there is hardly the same excuse for inaction.
Issuing from their gates can generally be
found some St. George valiant enough to
thrust his lance into the writhing body of
political ineptitude. And yet around places
as large as Stow-on-the-Wold the burgeoning
of a new democratic life seems to be pre-
vented at every turn. We find, for instance,
a wood-feller named Gabriel, of Icomb, unable
to obtain a holding after several years of
waiting. Here is a man, a typical countryman, skilled in wood-lore and a craftsman

of the fields, after many years of arduous labour acquiring a capital of £200. Such a man one would imagine any County Council would welcome as an approved applicant. Even he, though, has been denied access to the land. Perhaps this is not to be so wondered at when we hear how any break for freedom is thwarted amid these lonely hills.

Not far from Stow-on-the-Wold stands a village where seventeen men made application for small holdings. Most of these men knew what they could do with the land, for they were already allotment-holders, but some County Councillor took upon himself the task of coming down to the village and lecturing the men on the folly of their ways. Surely farmers, he told them, had enough trouble to make both ends meet. Did they want to buy trouble? Still the men did not withdraw their application, and whilst their application remained in the hands of the land-agent no less than three farms, I am told, came into the market in the same neighbourhood, yet the County Council failed to purchase any one of them. I do not think it even made a bid. Unfortunately, one of these farms contained the land rented by the allotment-holders, and this very farm was purchased by a person who had exhibited a strong animosity to small-holders. He immediately gave the allotment-holders notice to quit, and the applicants for small holdings, feeling that they might lose the chance of obtaining allotments on another farm, were cowed into submission and incontinently withdrew their applications.

The women, though, in a neighbouring village, showed a braver spirit when the village pound of Dorrington was fenced in by a private owner. They rose in a body and broke down its walls.

On leaving Stow-on-the-Wold I made Campden my headquarters. Here surely was a place, I thought, where those who toil in the fields might be able to breathe more freely, for was it not the country home of the Arts and Crafts Guild, a place where men, animated by high ideals, possessed minds astir with the spirit of modernity?

Such a hold, though, has feudalism taken on this mediæval village which lies at the gates of the Gainsborough estate, and at the foot of the hills owned by the Earls of Harrowby, who enclosed the large common which once stretched from Dover's Hill to Weston Subedge, that even the infusion of men from London and Glasgow with democratic ideals has failed to cause more than a ripple in this stagnant pool of mediævalism.

New cottages are badly wanted here, but, in spite of dark alleys redolent with smells that reach back to a lost ancestry, no new cottages appear save a group originally built for craftsmen. In spite of the fact that on many a farm the land is so poorly tilled that only one man is kept to the hundred acres, no land is by the public effort available for labourers—no land, that is, except some strips for allotments portioned out like meat at a workhouse dinner. It is left to an American citizen, the enterprising Mr. Fels, to purchase some seventy acres for the craftsmen and those who care to join them in tilling the land.

An application was sent in, I learn, when the Small Holdings Act became law, by men quite qualified to till the earth which their feet rarely left. The County Council approved of the applicants, but some gorgeously apparelled individual, descending from, heaven knows where, in a large motor car, pulled up at the "Lygon Arms," saw the agent of the Earl, and was heard to say, "The demand for small holdings is purely factitious, is it not?" "Exactly," replied the agent. "I thought so," said this gorgeous individual, who drove away, burying many labourers' hopes under his ponderous perspicacity.

One election only by ballot for the Parish

Council has, I believe, taken place in the last ten years. This state of things results in the large farmers and the publicans holding firmly to the necks of the old bottles and successfully resisting the pouring into them of new wine.

Much poverty haunts the dark alleys of the broad high street of mediæval Chipping Campden. Some residents, I am told, find æsthetic enjoyment at the sight of ragged boys and girls. They find it in the spectacle of the Catholic priest shepherding his ragged flock in the broad High Street ; and in the musty, old-world atmosphere that pervades the whole town. Had they to live the lives of the poor here perhaps they would not find this mediæval note of Campden charming either to their eyes or to their stomachs. Yet in spite of this poverty, in spite of wages being so low that the elbow-strength of a charwoman can be purchased for 6*d*. for the whole forenoon, and a labourer's muscles for 2*s*. a day, the landlords fail not to turn unceasingly the economic screw.

I know of a widow woman who, after twenty-two years' tenancy of a cottage of which the rent was once 1*s*. 9*d*., has had it raised from 2*s*. 3*d*. to 2*s*. 6*d*. because in one stuffy room she had a small fixed window made to open. This housing reform was, I believe, promised to her twenty years ago. It has now been accomplished at a permanent charge of 3*d.* a week.

You can easily discourage a countryman by a dose of official cold water, especially if he has been continuously under-fed and living continuously under the heel of a rural despotism. And this is what has happened at Campden. I was determined, though, to hearten them if I could, and so I asked one or two craftsmen to get up a meeting for me, which they did with generous alacrity.

Although it was the month of May when men do not like to leave their gardens in the evening, no less than seventy labourers assembled out of an audience of ninety. A local, trusted minister took the chair, and yet at the end of the meeting neither his nor my own efforts in the art of persuasion could get one of these men openly to voice their desires.

Eventually, the chairman asked all those who would form a branch of the National Land and Home League to hold up their hands. Ten hands only went up, of which several belonged to the craftsmen. I was disappointed. I felt I had been a failure. As I left the schoolroom, an American gentleman, a professor of Greek at a University in California, came up to me and said to me very kindly :

" Your address interested me immensely."

" But the men ? " I said. " What about
the men ? Not one of them said a word.
What would you feel if, after trying to probe
to the depths, nothing stirred ? "

" Ah ! " said the professor, "we have nothing
like your English countrymen in the United
States. To galvanise *these* men into life is the
finest work any English reformer can undertake.
It *must* be done, to save the old country."

The next day I heard that one or two farmers
who were Councillors were a little agitated
over the meeting, and that the labourers,
being aware of their presence or of that of
their informers, were afraid either to hold
up their hands or to speak. (Yet Englishmen continue to boast of their freedom !)
In the road, though, and along the lanes the
men, safe from the range of the employer's eye,
would speak to me. In a very short time
the membership increased from ten to fifty.

One of the men told me of a stockman
who had seven days a week at work for 13s.,
and that there were many men in that neighbourhood whose wages, after making deduc-
tions for wet days, did not amount to 10s. a
week. It was only by feeding their children
on bread and lard and on gifts of charity that
they were able to keep body and soul together.

Many labourers here are prohibited from
keeping pigs and hens in their cottage gardens,

6

because their employer-landlords, who pay
them such wretchedly low wages, fear that
the men may be tempted to dip their hands
into the corn-bins at the farms.

Under such conditions of life no one
should be in the least surprised at the gross
form of vice that runs riot in certain
blocks of cottages, where every doorstep
seems a tombstone, crushing every spiritual
endeavour. So dominated are the lives
of the men and the women of the poorest
class by the rich, that it was seriously proposed at a nursing association that the parish
nurse should not be allowed to visit girls who
gave birth to illegitimate children!

That such a state of things exists to-day,
in the twentieth century, makes one pause to
wonder whether the labourer was not in-
finitely better off before the common land
on Dover's Hill and Weston Subedge was
enclosed in 1850, that is, before the Earls of
Harrowby had a passion for high farming.
We learn, for instance, from the *Fieldsman's
Book*, that a certain Giles Cockbill received
from 1841 up to 1850 his 10s. a week " and
his pair of stout shoes " for acting as hayward
to the common fields, the duties of which
consisted of clearing the common, furzing,
repairing mounds, and cleaning out the pools
in the cow-pasture. He then paid, as a

peasant small-holder, 7s. a year rent for his little holding of 2 roods and 17 poles. His status seems to have been that of a small farmer, for the record of the *Fieldsman's Book* is presumptive evidence that the farmer and the labourer were often interchangeable terms. Many labourers called themselves farmers, and many sons of farmers called themselves labourers. The class-cleavage appears to have been less apparent then than now.

Of the forty-three names of the Weston labourers on the enclosure award of 1852, only eight can now be traced, representing fifteen families in all. All that was left for the poor of the 1,884 acres enclosed was four acres, and I understand that, as the poor were unable to pay for the fencing of these four acres, the lawyer who undertook to fence it for them did it at an annual charge of 7 per cent. of the capital expended! As this capital charge has never been paid off, a tribute is still being paid to a certain family who inherited the lawyer's wealth.

No longer can the men of the Cotswolds sing the old commoner's song along with the men of Dartmoor:

> Rushes vur datching, turve to burn,
> An' stone vur walls so strong.
> Plenty o' kaip vur bullocks and shaip
> To the Dartmoor man belong.

On the whole, then, it is difficult to see in what way the present Giles Cockbills are better off than the Giles Cockbills of 1850. Many of them get no more than 10s. a week wages, out of which rent will be a larger item to be deducted than it was in 1850. No one to-day gives them stout pairs of shoes besides their wages, and if they hire land they have to pay three times the rent paid by their forbears.

3. *A Pastoral of Oxfordshire*

The village is that of W——, which lies not far remote from a city of great learning. It is a village owned almost entirely by the Lord of the Manor.

It was here that a friend of mine got to know Enoch Young, who is the secretary of the Village Land Club, and the backbone of a struggling little Nonconformist community. In every sense of the word he represented the best type of the village labourer.

Enoch told in a few simple words the story of his life—the life of a poor man who strove honestly to maintain the traditions of England's bold peasantry.

"Take my own case," he said: "time and time again I have decided to quit the old place, and make a home where a man may be a man, and think what he likes without fear of the consequences.

" My folks have lived in this village for generations, and we should have been a lot better off to-day if we hadn't made the mistake of having our own opinions, instead of sharing those of the squire. I mind what my own father had to put up with on account of his independence. He was, though I say it, a man who, although he had very little education, thought a lot about the right and wrong of things ; and this doesn't help a working man in a village to be contented with his lot. When I was a lad, my father's wage was 9s. 6d. a week, out of which he had to pay house-rent and keep a family of seven. He was a very steady man, was my father ; in fact he couldn't well be any other, on a wage of that sort ; but with all his carefulness, you can guess it was hard work for us to keep body and soul together.

" Well, when Joe Arch started his movement to band the labourers together, my father joined the Union. Most of the other men in the village did the same ; but it wasn't long before the local farmers ordered the men to break away from the Union. My father was about the only man in the parish who stood firm, and the result was that he was very soon out of a job.

" He was a good, all-round, useful man, who understood his work, but that didn't matter. For nearly two years he could get no regular work ; farmer after farmer refused to have anything to do with him, and all he could get to do were casual jobs.

" I've heard my mother say that he never earned more than seven shillings during any one week of this time. I was only a little lad then, but the very thought of those days makes me shudder even now ; I expect it was that which sort of sowed the seeds of rebellion in me. How we got through that time I can hardly tell you. The strain and the stress of it all broke my mother up, and hastened my father's end. I worked on a farm myself up to about ten years ago, when, as I could see no outlook in that line, I decided to take the village carrier's business, which was then vacant. I got along all right for a bit, and pulled together a very good business, though the fact that I was a chapel man always seemed to stand in my way.

" After I had been in business about two years, I happened to go one night to an open-air Tariff Reform meeting, which was held on our green, and at the end I put one or two simple questions to the speakers. Of course I left no doubt open as to my being a Free Trader ; anyhow, when I called the next morning at one of the biggest farmer's here for a hamper, which I used to take every week to a laundry at O———, I was told that someone else had taken it, and there was no need for me to call again.

"One after another my bigger customers treated me in the same way, and the bulk of my business soon disappeared. Those were my darkest days ; and if it had not been for the entreaties of my wife I should have cleared out. One day, when things were about at their blackest, and I was well-nigh despairing, I passed the home in which my brave old father had lived, and as I thought of all he'd gone through, and what my mother had suffered, I vowed I'd stay and see things through. Soon after that the Small Holdings Act was passed, and I applied for a bit of land. After a lot of trouble I got it, but it's about a mile and a half away from my home, and so it is not half so profitable to me as it might be. If I could get a house on the holding I'd be a made man, and able to shake my fist at those who would crush the likes of me ; but they know that as well as I do, and I don't see much hopes of a house at present. I am not an old man, but I've seen some of the likeliest fellows and smartest girls leave this parish, as they saw no chance of getting on.

" A man mustn't think for himself in a village. If he does he invites beggary. Nobody knows the dreary life a villager lives, save those who endure it. What's a man to look forward to in this village? A tumbledown cottage at a high rent, and a miserable wage of about 13s. for a week's hard work ; no place of social gathering but the public house, and no chance of improving himself in any way—that's what life means in an English village. Do you wonder after this that our best class of young man packs up and goes to Canada ? When I think about these things I am well-nigh tempted to go there myself. And let me tell you one thing more : it's no use you giving us a vote, unless you give us a chance to get on the land, and find us a decent roof over our heads. But it is difficult to speak of these things in an open way," he said with a profound sigh. "To talk of cottage folks' hardships in a village only makes life harder for them as well as for me ; and the worst of it all is, the more they are left alone the less they care. If a man does not care about being lifted out of the mire it is tremendously hard to lift him. Is it any wonder he sits half asleep in the alehouse ? "

4. *A Pastoral of Wiltshire*

This village, too, lies not very far removed from an educational centre. Indeed, some of its land, as well as its insanitary cottages, is owned by colleges and even hospitals !

The speaker is a man very well known to me, and much respected in his own village. He is a teetotaller, and exceedingly thrifty. Starting life as a farmer's boy, he has now become a mechanic. As a craftsman I think he is a genius.

I will let him tell the story of his life in the naked simplicity of his own words. A tallow candle stood burning on the deal table of the dimly lighted, stone-flagged living-room of the thatched cottage, which served as the entertainment-hall for friends and the nursery of the children.

" The first thing I remember is living in a barn (it is straight in front of the cottage where I now live), for there was no cottage of any sort for us to get into. We then, as soon as a chance occurred, went to a tied cottage on a small farm where my father worked for 8s. a week.

" When I was seven years old I went out to drive the horses at plough, and my father agreed verbally with the master that I was to have £3 for my work for the first year ;

after this they both agreed to leave my
pay in the master's keeping till I was old
enough to be apprenticed to some trade.
After five years the master died, and as
there was no written agreement to show,
the executors took no notice of my father's
claim. Thus I worked my first five years
for nothing.

" The farm was then thrown in with an
adjoining large farm where my father had to
work, and I was sent to school, as my father
now saw the folly of putting me to work so
young, and wanted to give me a chance to
learn my letters. I hadn't been at school
about two months before the new master
wanted me to work for him. Dad told him
he should like me to remain at school for a
year or so, but the master replied, ' If he had
boys living in his cottages they must work
for him if he wanted them.' So that settled
the case, and I went to work again at 2s. 6d. a
week (quite a big rise !). I remember looking
after the pigs in the fields after the corn had
been carried, and also minding the sheep on
Sundays as well as week-days, and for Sundays
I was allowed to take my ' tommy-bag ' to
the farmhouse to have some odds-and-ends of
food put in it. Sometimes there were some
little bits of bacon or a bit of ham-bone put
in, and, my lads ! it was a treat in those

days, as we hardly ever had a bit of bacon at home : bread and lard, and sometimes salt butter, was the chief victuals we could get. As for butcher's meat, we never even saw it. One day I and the carter were out with the horses and wagon, and for some reason or other the horses took fright and ran away (after knocking me sprawling into the ditch), and broke the wagon and harness badly. The master, after threatening the carter for letting the horses run away, came to me when alone and asked me how it was they ran away. I said I thought a bird or something must have frightened them, but he was very angry, and said I had no business to *think*; but this only made me think all the more.

" A year or two after this I was put to milk the cows, and took the milk to the station. My eyes began to open, and I grumbled at dad for not getting me more than 5s. a week. I had to start at 4.30 in the morning, and was not done till 6 p.m. So dad said I must agree with the master myself for the future (we were hired by the year then). When Michaelmas came I asked the master for a rise to 7s. 6d. a week, as I was going to do the same work as he had been paying 7s. 6d. for to the chap that was leaving. He said he should **do nothing of the sort, and if I did not choose** to come to his terms—6s. 6d.—I was to get out of the house, *and my father too*. I told dad of this, and he said I must please myself. Knowing my father was an old man and his work nearly done, I went next evening cap in hand to the master and said, ' Please, sir, I will come to your terms.'

" This went on for a few years, my wages gradually rising till I got 10s. a week and was second milker. About this time, strange to say both master and my father fell ill.

" One day in harvest-time we had only three men instead of four to milk the cows, and consequently took longer time to do it. This so exasperated the foreman on the farm that, after swearing at and bullying me as long as he liked, he said, as a finishing touch, ' Thee canst only just keep a house over thy old father's head now, and thee won't do that much longer if thee doesn't look out ' (bitter pill, that !). I made no answer, but bucked into the work and tried to forget it.

" The master and dad both died shortly, and I was free, but like a bird with his wings clipped. Several bills were owing in dad's name (something like £5), as he had been ill a whole year, and the Parish, after he had been working in the district all his life (sometimes for 6s. a week), allowed him only a gallon of bread and 6*d.* a week. I made up my mind that the bills should be paid. I agreed to stay on another year for 11*s.* a week. I saved enough out of this and my over-money to pay off the debt. I then agreed to stay on one more year for 12*s.* a week and £3 over. I saved £7 out of this, and then felt I could stand on my own feet.

" The following year the foreman asked me to stay on again, saying it would be a bad job for me if I should be out of work all the winter. I thanked him, looked him up and down, and reminded him I was free, and had no old father to keep, and I would thank him for a reference for the past eight years' service. This he gave me, with instructions to hand it to my next employer, ' as a man, ' he said, ' might be a blackguard later on,' and he did not want to be referred to again. To this I simply said, ' Thank you,' and good-bye to farm labour for ever."

This was his story, told with the sincere and splendid simplicity of one unversed in letters. But it saddened me to note, in the light of the flickering candle guttering in the draughts of gaping cracks, the hectic flush on his cheeks, the feverish brilliance of eyes that had burnt up life quickly, telling how the disease which consumes those who were too long ill-nourished in childhood had marked him too as its victim.

5. *A Pastoral of Hampshire*

When Leonora Partridge stepped into the tastefully furnished kitchen of her little country home, which nestled in the lap of the North Downs, her maid, a girl of sixteen, with sweet blue eyes and light brown hair, looked up from her task of cleaning the linoleum and uttered these words :

" Lizzie Turner's been and disgraiced 'erself."

Leonora Partridge gasped. She almost bowed her gentle, stately head before this onslaught ; this callous, brutal judgment on a frail and suffering sister, pronounced from the lips of her own sweet little maid—a mere child in years.

" What, dear ? " asked Leonora, in a tone of gentle rebuke.

Rosie wrung out her cloth in the pail, briskly flicked a straying tress of her silky brown hair with her hand, and repeated :

" Lizzie Turner's been and disgraiced 'erself. She've got to leave Redlands."

Ever since Leonora had possessed a home of her own she had made a point of getting her young maid-servants to regard her as

a personal friend. A woman of culture,
separated by many a class-barrier from those
she wished especially to befriend, she had
yet insisted that they should regard her as
a sister, an older sister, endowed with greater
social responsibilities, for which she would
have to render full account to her Maker.

" She 'ave got to get married at once,"
pursued Rosie, without a blush.

" But, dear child, you should not judge
her—you must not say that she has dis-
graced herself," said Leonora reproachfully.

" Well, that's what Auntie Bertha says—
and she attends chapel reg'lar, she do,"
answered Rosie, defending herself, and splash-
ing a good deal of water about.

" Your Aunt Bertha is a very good woman,
Rosie, but our Saviour never judged any
woman like that," said Leonora a little
stiffly, for she was a churchwoman. " If
Lizzie and her man are going to marry, I
do not see where the disgrace comes in."

Rosie looked up with wide-open eyes of
astonishment at her mistress, into whose
cheeks a little colour came and went like a
pale, flickering flame.

Had she said a rash thing, Leonora asked
herself ? So many of these agricultural
labourers were fathers before they were
married ; yet it was surely better to ac-

knowledge it openly as the sacred consum-
mation of love! She felt that what she
had said was true ; but was it wise to blurt
out the truth to the uneducated ? She
wished she could find a wise friend—a priest ?
No, not a priest : she was a good Protestant.
She thought of the vicar's wife, and immediately the corners of her mouth dropped.

"But she won't get no 'ome of 'er own in
this parish," pursued the world-wise maiden
to her gentle mistress.

Ah, that was the rub! Rosie had driven
her point home ; for it was not only the
sudden revelation of Rosie's Eve-like knowledge which had made Leonora gasp, it was
also the flashing thought of the edict passed
on all girls in trouble who lived within the
borders of the Great Estate. Ever since
Lady Venables had reigned supreme as
mistress, it had become an unwritten law that
no cottage accommodation should be found
for couples with children born out of wedlock.
Even if this young couple were marshalled
off to church in time, there was still the question of a home to be solved. Leonora knew
that at that moment there was not a single
empty cottage in the parish, and Sir Henry
had declared that he would not build any
because they "spoilt the look of the place."

Leonora did not ask her man to harness

the ginger-coloured pony to the old-fashioned chaise, but, drawing on her gloves with meticulous care and adjusting her goloshes—for she was aware of the muddy entrance to Redlands Farm—she betook herself thither on foot. All along the lane, on one side of which rooks were pillaging the winter-sown wheat, she thought of the gloomy household at Redlands ; the weak, easy-going, florid farmer, who invariably came home drunk on market days ; the gaunt, hard-featured woman—his second wife—with a granite-like puritanism, on whose marriage two sons and the only daughter had left the farm, never to return ; and of the one son who remained, rarely speaking to his stepmother, and quarrelling daily with his father. His ineptitude indoors resulted in his banishment to the scullery for his meals, where he took them with Lizzie, who was a distant relative of the family. Out of doors his slight mental deficiency led to each day being begun by quarrels between father and son if they happened to be doing any work in common. Of late these quarrels had become more violent in character. Tom, or Long Tom as the villagers called him, was a man of great height and strength, and as his father grew older, and physically more feeble, the son asserted himself with greater determination.

7

The picturesque farmhouse with its stone
slab tiles, green and grey with lichen and
moss, its damp red walls built up between
old oak beams, came into sight. Right in
front of the house was the farmyard, a
mire of sodden manure ; and in the middle
of it lay a pool which, touched by the rays
of the declining sun, glowed with a sombre
light. Leonora fancied it looked red—blood-
red ; but it was only liquid manure into which
some drops of blood had flowed, for close by
stood the hog-stool and tub. Evidently a
pig had just been killed. Leonora had to
gather up her skirts to step over the puddle
before the little gate with the awkward latch
which opened on to the path of flag-stones
leading to the front door. As she passed
she observed the figure of Mr. Steer, the
farmer, leaning over the rounded wall of the
pigstye. She noted his quaint old form
clothed in a dun-coloured coat ; his battered
billycock hat at the back of his head of iron-
grey hair ; his florid face ; and, sticking out
of a side pocket of his loose, crumpled coat,
the tails of a pair of kippers. This tickled
her fancy so much that, from having felt on
the point of crying, she now began to laugh.
Three mud-bespattered ducks, emerging from
the mire of the yard, crossed her pathway.
She heard Steer say, as though it were said

with a sigh: " Well, I dunno', I think I shall keep that there bar pig . . . "

Then she knocked at the door.

When, at the end of an hour, Leonora emerged from the dark porch shrouded by a crimson rambler, her kind grey eyes shone with a great light. She was pale, but she had triumphed over the hard-featured woman and the slightly inebriated husband who had come in and taken part in the discussion.

Mrs. Steer had shown her fear of giving offence to Lady Venables, and possibly to the vicar's wife, who generally saw that her ladyship's orders were carried out. After what had happened she feared that, if she kept the young couple under her roof, she might be accused of condoning the sin, even though they were about to be married in church. Leonora had pointed out that there was no empty cottage to be had in the parish, and that it would mean that the young couple would have to leave the neighbourhood. She was listened to with respect, for she was acknowledged to belong to " the gentry " ; moreover, she was a customer of Steer's, who performed certain little farming operations for her. He threw in his entire weight on the side of Leonora, declaring that he would never get a cheaper labourer than Steve Bond, who had come up from the Shires to " live in " with them, and was a good worker. And as for the young hussy—well, she too could be kept on as a cheap servant.

As Leonora picked her way over the flag-stones she heard the gate click sharply. Looking up she saw the vicar's wife, who, though she bowed with cordiality, passed with a searching, rapier-like glance from her cold blue eyes.

Three days afterwards two men in flame-coloured coats were riding at their ease along the Redlands lane. Their hunters were smoking, for they were returning home after a hard day's ride across country. In front ran the hounds with the Whips, and the long, muddy lane with its gleaming cart-rucks was broken by this splash of mottled colour. The taller horseman was leisurely lighting a cigar as in the twilight they drew towards Redlands Farm, which looked sombre as they approached it. He was comfortably tired. The world went very well with him whilst there was something to hunt in these degenerate days, for was he not Sir Henry Vernon Boscawen Venables, Bart.—to give him his full title—which, however, among the sporting yokels was too often abbreviated to " old 'Arry." By his side rode his intimate friend, John Sandiman. Though now middle-aged,

the two had been close friends since their
undergraduate days at Christ Church.

" How is that affair getting on ? " asked
John Sandiman, pointing with his riding-
stock towards the black barn of Redlands,
which overshadowed the road.

Sir Henry drew his cigar from his lips and,
shrugging his shoulders, said :

" Oh, that's Honor's affair, not mine. I've
got enough to do to look after the stables and
the kennels, and that's a bit of a job sometimes—to keep the pack up to the scratch.
Other cattle—cottage folk—is Honor's domain
and, after all, what can you expect
when you shut up a young stallion in the
yard with a filly ! The girl, I understand,
has to clear."

A screech-owl passed overhead in the dusky
November twilight.

" There's a tragic gloom about the place
somehow," observed Sir Henry's friend.

" It's that cursed yard," said the other,
rather irritably. " I must have it altered : it
comes right flush with the road, and the
ammonia coming from it is enough to make
the bare road itself fertile soil. Look at that
pool of liquid manure ! How these farmers
waste valuable material ! . . . But don't think,
Jack, that this business of refusing cottage
accommodation to couples with illegitimate

kids is anything to do with me. I'm no saint, nor am I a damned hypocrite. It's a rum thing," he went on ruminatingly, " that if you go through those doors first "—he pointed to the church steeple—" you are quite virtuous, but if you walk through that churchyard with a girl on your arm afterwards, it's hell to pay."

" It's hell to pay sometimes if you go through the doors first," muttered the other. " Do you ever think of Mollie, Harry ? "

Sir Henry flung the red-tipped cigar from his mouth as though it had a bitter taste.

" Of course I do," he answered brusquely, " and of the kid, too. I wonder if he knows about me ? I wonder if I have ever met him, and what he thinks of me. . . . I say, Jack, let's drop it. Everything seems confoundedly weird to-night, near this gloomy homestead. I want my dinner. We'll have up some of that old port." He touched up his horse sharply, and the deepening twilight engulfed them.

Before the week was over the affair had taken a dramatic turn. Revolt against the moral dominion of Lady Venables had reared its head in an unexpected quarter. That patient hind, Stephen Bond, fretting under the galling yoke of a self-constituted committee of parochial ladies, had suddenly

turned doggedly obstinate. It was said that
he actually swore before the vicar's wife,
declaring that no one should interfere between
him and his wife—he had the audacity to
call Lizzie his wife! When Lizzie was told
by Mrs. Steer that she would have to leave
the farmhouse immediately, Steve declared
he would go with her, that he would take
her right away from the parish and get
married in town and never come back any
more to the country. In town, he had heard,
there was freedom; and there big folk did
not poke their noses into your business.
Steve demanded his money on Friday morning, and by the afternoon he and Lizzie stood
outside the farm gate, waiting for the farm
cart which was to take them to the railway
station with their one box.

Another pig had been killed that morning,
and its blood again stained to a dark red
the pool of liquid manure in the farmyard.
Quarrels between Steer and his son had been
incessant during the week, growing more and
more violent; for Tom, who had a warm
heart and was really attached to Lizzie, was
righteously angry at her being turned out of
the house. Father and son were now lifting
the dead pig into the market cart. It had
been arranged that Steve, Lizzie, and Tom
should ride together to the station with the

pig. At the last moment, Steer would be able to make use of Steve's services by getting him to help Tom to unload the pig.

Steve was lifting the pathetic little deal box, which contained Lizzie's and his own entire worldly goods, on to his shoulder, when he heard father and son break out quarrelling as usual as to how a dead pig should be lifted into a cart. Steve, who was very near breaking-point, turned to Steer and said:

" I'll walk, thank 'ee — come on, Liz. Good-bye, Tom."

Tom suddenly let go of the pig, dropping its white hind legs over the tail-board of the cart.

" Good-bye, Steve! good-bye, Liz!" he shouted after them excitedly, watching Steve walking away with the little box on his shoulder, and Lizzie by his side holding his arm.

" They never shook hands with us—they never shook hands with us," exclaimed Tom wildly to his father. " Look, there is blood on our hands—blood!"

" Put the pig in, you damned fool," said the father angrily.

" Put the bloody pig in yourself," retorted Tom. " You turned them out, you let them go—you turned Liz out on the roads—you damned old scoundrel."

Steer lifted his hand and struck his son full in the face. They closed with one another, striking out fiercely, blow after blow, and lurching forward, stumbled over a muck heap, and rolled down to the edge of the pool of liquid manure. The first to rise, Tom, with an oath, flung his father into the middle of the murky pool ; and there he lay, quite still, his iron-grey hair matted in the muddy compound, his toes turned upwards, and his eyes fixed in a glassy stare in the direction of the blanched hind legs of the pig, which was still hanging over the tail-board of the cart.

At that moment Sir Henry Vernon Boscawen Venables and her ladyship were walking towards the farm to discover for themselves if success had crowned her ladyship's efforts to establish a Code of Morality. Nearing the homestead she saw to her amazement Steve and Lizzie together walking away from it. As she faced them she stopped and said to them :

" Where are you going ? "

For answer she received a stony stare from Steve, who passed on his way with the box on his shoulder, and Lizzie clinging to his side.

It was the first time in her life that Lady Venables had been snubbed. She had been cut by a " common labourer." Sir Henry frowned as he looked furtively at his wife's flushed face.

" What is the meaning of all this ? " she said.

" Rural depopulation," answered her husband, lamely attempting a joke. " The town will get the increase."

Pillowed in poverty, cradled in some reeking, drink-sodden slum, would the Babe first open its wondering eyes. Better far some manger over which the lark might herald childhood's divinity. But Sir Henry was not thinking of this. His mind was dwelling on his wife's Roman nose, and her cold, thin lips.

As they approached the homestead it seemed lifeless. The farmyard gate stood wide open, but no one appeared to be working. Then a horrible scene smote Lady Venables' eyes. She saw the figure of old Steer lying on his back, with eyes fixed in a glassy stare—lying quite still in the pool.

" Look ! " she exclaimed, touching her husband's arm.

Tom was sitting on the hog-stool, muttering wild words as he gazed at his father.

Sir Henry stepped forward.

" What's this ? " he cried in a stern voice. Tom looked up with a strange, wild light in his eyes ; his long, dishevelled hair hanging over his face.

" This ! " he shouted, rising from the stool and pointing at the prostrate form, " this be poor old feyther ; blind drunk. Look at his eyes—the drunken old sweep ! He turned Lizzie out on the road—that's what he did —blind drunk, that's what he is. Look at his eyes ! . . . Oh, it's old 'Arry, Sir 'Enery—beg pardon. Steve'll stick to her ; he'll be truer to his wife than ever you've been to yourn, Arry. I've 'eard tell about you. Ah, my lady, there's been foul play here. Is your hand white ?—white as that pig's back ? Or is it red with blood like mine—blood red ! blood red ! "

He sank down on the hog-stool and wept like a child.

6. *A Pastoral of Dorset*

On a lonely shore of the West Country which has little or no site value, a tiny stone cottage was built by a fisherman eighty years ago. He built it with his own hands, and lived in it without paying any rent. Then he died, leaving the cottage to his son, who in his turn lived in it for sixty-four years without paying any rent whatever. But the landlord who owned the surrounding land also had a son, who, on inheriting, meanly demanded a tribute of one shilling a year. This the cottager stoutly refused, fearing, like many other squatters, the first turn of an economic screw which never ceases to turn until it drives the occupier completely out of his own homestead. The landlord persisted in claiming the shilling. He threatened the cottager for a whole year ; but the cottager being a widower, having no wife or child to keep, and living entirely alone, held out with grim determination.

Surely life had brought so few sweets to this poor man, robbed of his wife, childless, and destitute of the solace of intimate comradeship, that he might have been left in peace in his lonely hut and allowed to live to the end of his old age in humble isolation ? But the landlord decided to evict him.

He sent his hirelings one day when the old man was out fishing in his boat to win his daily maintenance. When the fisherman returned and beached his boat on the soil of free England he found that he had only returned from winning his daily bread to see his furniture in a ditch and the windows and doors of his cottage boarded up against him.

Broken-hearted, and like one bereft of his senses, he wandered about on the Downs until he was arrested for vagrancy and taken to the workhouse eight miles away. He escaped, and returned once more to his own beloved shore, the stones of which his feet had trodden for sixty-four years. Unable to gain entrance to his cottage, he lived under an overhanging cliff, difficult of access, where kindly cottagers who visited him from a distance brought him gifts of food at night. His mind was said to have become unhinged, and after three months' exposure on this wild cliff he was found dead one day, sitting upright under an old apple tree planted by his father in his own cottage garden.

Throughout the whole of this drama, right up to its tragic end, the landlord lived quite near. Again was man crucified : this time it was on the white cliffs of a " civilised " land, nineteen hundred years after the Redeemer was nailed to the Cross.

7. *A Pastoral of Surrey*

I

As he lifted his adze to cleave a hoop in the heart of the Tanhurst woods, his quick woodman's ear heard the distant rustle of dead leaves. It was not, he knew, a rabbit scurrying through the underwood, nor was it the noisy patter of the blackbird or pheasant. It was someone coming towards him. It could not be his mate, old Ned

Lipscombe, for he had that lopping, lethargic tread of the land-worker. These footfalls were as light and as rapid as a wood-nymph's.

"Cooey!" rang out a musical feminine voice, and from out of the uncut hazel stepped a dainty figure in a nurse-girl's dress.

A flush mounted to Martin's handsome brown face. It was Trixy, or, as she now preferred to be called, Beatrice Lipscombe.

He shyly dug his adze into the upright stake on which he was cleaving hoops, and stepped out into the broke with a quickened heart-beat to meet his sweetheart, who, however, remained quite self-possessed. How dainty she looked in her little fur cap!

"My people have gone to Egypt, Martin," she said, shaking hands with him demurely. She always spoke of the family at Tanhurst Place, where she was nurse to Lady Chard's son and heir, as "my people." Her little hand was lost within the folds of his mighty grip. His wide-opened nostrils inhaled a faint perfume of violets as she stood close to him.

"Isn't it sweet, Martin? I shall be at home on board wages the whole of January. Oh dear! how romantic it is here!" she prattled on, opening her big eyes widely. "This dear little hut, with your roof of shavings and your pot slung over the wood fire! Martin,

I shall cook your dinner for you! Oh dear, I believe I have forgotten how to cook! It's so quiet and sheltered here. Outside the wood the east wind is piercing. Ugh!" She shuddered at the thought of the bleak outside world.

Martin watched her lithesome figure move gracefully towards the little wood fire built on the leeward side of his hut, of which the back and windward sides were built up of faggots and hurdles. Martin noted how white her hands were now as she took off her gloves with deliberation.

" Ain't you glad to see me again, Martin ? " she asked him as he remained standing silent.

" Glad!—you know that. But you are different, Trixy." He blurted out these last words as he stood outside the hut watching her movements.

" Different ! What nonsense ! Well, I suppose we all alter a little—for the good, I hope," she added, with a ladylike primness.

" You are different," persisted the young woodman, "that is, since you've been up at the Big House," he added, with a glowering stare towards its distant towers. He stood there in his ragged sleeves, handsome but perspiring after his onslaught at shaving hoops on the stool—or brake as he called it.

Trixy was well aware that she had altered,

and she was proud of the difference. Her clothes were more becoming, and her speech had been pruned of nearly all its local peculiarities. The exfoliation had rapidly progressed under her ladyship's exquisite and sensitive ear. The accent of the future Sir Kenneth, even of his baby lips, must be safeguarded. It pleased Trixy that Martin should notice all these subtle changes, but at the same time she resented being told that she was different. Martin ought to have taken that for granted.

" If you mean by different," she said tartly, looking at the wood embers and speaking with emphasized precision, " more polish, of course one gets that by mixing with the aristocracy, and that's an improvement, ain't it, Martin ? "

" It depends upon the material," he answered slowly and thoughtfully. " Now oak oughter remain as rough as it's hewn."

" I'm sorry," she said, drawing herself up haughtily, " that you do not think I have improved. I may as well tell you now, Martin, that I wish you would call me Beatrice in future instead of Trixy. I don't ask you to call me Miss Lipscombe because we are such old friends, but I do ask you to drop the Trixy."

" Be-at-Beatrice ! Why it sounds like

play-acting, don't it ? All right, Trixy, I
will if you fancies it. I told you you were
different." He sighed, and, standing at his
brake, with wrists like supple steel, he began
shredding hoop after hoop.

"What do you get for them—for those
hoops ? " asked Trixy, looking round at his
neat, naked bundles of white hoops bound with
withes of hazel.

Martin did not like being asked what he
got for his work, at least not by Trixy. It
seemed a question too gross to be asked by
those sweet lips of hers. If she had taken pride
in his skill apart from the payment of it, how
he would have answered all her questions with
enthusiasm !

"So much a gross, 'cording to different
sizes," he answered vaguely.

"How tiresome those stubs are ! " cried
Trixy, looking out towards where the underwood had been cut. "They do trip you up
so ! "

"Ah ! " answered the woodman. "Think
what a pretty carpet of primroses and blue-
bells and anemones I am laying bare for your
pretty little feet to tread upon as the spring
comes along."

When the spring comes ! The frost lay on
the rough lichen-covered branches of the oak
and clung to the smooth, purple stem of the

8

beech and hazel. A splash of mid-day sun, the only possible one at this time of the year in the wood, lit up for a moment the clearing. A robin hopped about on a heap of Martin's shavings and wanted to peer into his pot, but feared the stranger in the fur cap. Martin's coat and the skin of a rabbit were hanging up in the shed ; the rabbit was in the pot. Trixy glanced at it and then rose.

" If you don't choose to tell of your earnings, I don't mind. It has nothing to do with me, I'm sure ! "

" Don't you git hitchin' at me about nothing, Trixy," protested Martin. " If you will sit there, I'll tell you what I makes on all my work. . . . There's a cantata to-morrow night at the chapel, Trixy."

" Are you playing, Martin ? " asked the girl, hesitating as to whether she should go or not.

" Yes. A violin solo," he answered with simplicity.

At this moment the sound of crackling branches broke upon their ears, and a smartly dressed young man, arrayed in leggings and riding-breeches, appeared in the clearing. He looked towards the hut and began to whistle, till he caught sight of Trixy, and then he began leisurely to examine the oak trees left standing and marked for winter felling.

" It's the timber-merchant," muttered

Martin, getting up and walking towards Mr. Timothy Barrow.

"Good-bye," said Trixy to Martin, in a tone that she had learnt from her mistress.

Mr. Timothy Barrow lifted his cap as Trixy passed on through the wood. He stared at her vanishing figure and then, turning to Martin, said :

"Didn't know you kept such good company here, Martin. Sister, eh ? "

"No," answered Martin stolidly.

"Eh ? Oh, you sly dog! Devilish pretty, though——"

He was just about to dig Martin in the ribs in the familiar way in which he treated work-men when he wanted to get the better of a deal, but a light in Martin's eyes caused Mr. Barrow to drop his hand. He was a young man with a golden moustache, eyes too close together, and a loose lower lip. He gazed across the underwood and sighed. He tried to whistle, but failed.

II

A wedge of yellow light suddenly struck across the dark lane, illuminating the hedge and trees opposite, as the doors of the chapel were thrown open. A few noisy, giggling girls and callow youths bundled out first, and began to make catcalls. One or two of the older youths hung about hiding themselves in the deep shadows, waiting to dart out upon and sheepishly follow some bright-eyed girl as she became visible.

A tall figure holding a violin case in his hand came swinging out of the open door straight into the wedge of yellow light. It lanced a golden pathway before his feet. It was Martin Redwood. Close to him walked a clinging figure wrapped in a cloak, and a faint aroma of violets scented the crisp night air. Around the door this delicate perfume expired under the strong, pungent smell of shag. Martin stepped swiftly out of the broad path of light into the dark night that rose up like a wall of coal-dust on the edge of the tongue of light, and yet its country clarity was unmistakable.

The country lane is never really dark to the countryman. There is always a sombre glow of grey light about, even when the townsman calls it pitch-dark. Trixy slipped her little hand within Martin's arm. She had forgotten to put on her gloves ! Neither spoke ; they paced on together in silence. Music had emotion-alised both player and listener. He had looked into her soft eyes and swam in their liquid depths as she sat wrapped in dreamland. Martin had been applauded vociferously as he played with great expression on his cheap and indifferent violin. His was the triumph of the evening. Trixy dreamed of a swaying conductor's baton wielded by Martin instead of the slashing billhook ; of audiences breaking out into frenzied applause ; of an evening dress in place of a ragged shirt. It might be better than being a gamekeeper in velveteens.

How Martin remembered that walk ! Even now he can visualise it at any moment : how a great motor passed with flashing lamps which threw up before him the bare branches of the trees that seemed to spread out to him attenuated fingers of sympathy ; how some ducks, those wary night-watchmen, splashed into the roadside pond ; how chilly that splash sounded, and how warm was Trixy pressed against his side.

The lovers walked rapidly down the hill until they reached the darkest part of the lane, where a large stack of cordwood and faggots were piled up upon the roadside waste. Here Martin stopped and bent his head. Trixy instinctively raised her red lips to meet his. It was her immortal moment. Never again did she taste of the wine of life untainted with the lees. He too had captured life's exquisite moment and made it imperishably his own.

On a dull morning, a week afterwards, with a leaden sky overhead, Martin left his broke in the wood to select some special straight stems of hazel for withes. The cold weather had made it difficult to twist the brittle wood in wands for tying the bundles of hoops, and he had left a fire burning in his hut over which he would hold his withes in order to make them more pliable. He sang at his task, for love was in his heart, and he possessed that uncommon quality in a modern workman—joy in his work. He was fortunate in that, to some extent, he could choose his employment, for besides being skilled at the making of wattles, hurdles, and hoops, he could mow, reap, and thatch. He spent his whole year harvesting; in summer there was the hay and corn harvest; in winter he had the harvest of the woods to clear, the cutting of bean-sticks, pea-sticks, and poles from which he fashioned rake-handles and sneaths. In spring there was the felling of oaks and bark-stripping. He was known as an independent workman who could pick and choose both his work and his employer.

A moment later, as Martin was returning to his shed thatched with shavings, with an armful of hazels, he saw Trixy sitting by his fire. At her side stood the timber-merchant. Young Barrow was trying to hold her ungloved hand. Martin's heart stood still. Standing in a tense expectancy, he could hear the soughing of the wind in the trees overhead.

A frown bit into his bronzed forehead as he strode up to his sweetheart. Trixy's hand returned to her lap. Her cloak was thrown back, and the timber-merchant's small eyes were fixed upon her openwork bodice, which displayed her white neck. Martin noticed this as Barrow turned round and said : " I came to measure those oaks for planing in the spring, and so, whilst Miss Lipscombe is paying you a call, I will go round and have a look at them."

Martin answered nothing. Trixy fretfully fixed her eyes on the flameless wood embers. Martin sent his gaze across the wood, over the distant purple haze of beech and hazel, to the towering rookery behind which stood Tanhurst Place, dark and sinister.

" Martin," said Trixy slowly, " I wanted to have a talk with you. Are you always going to be a woodman ? People say you ought to be a musician."

" Sell my music for gold ? Scrape gut for coppers ? That I ain't ! "

" But what can you earn as a woodman ? "

" I can earn my crown a day at hurdle-making," he answered sullenly.

" But that is only for a short time, Martin, and, if you won't turn your musical talent to account, why not start a little business as a rake-maker, and sell them yourself ? "

" How am I to get the capital to start with ? 'Tain't any good nowadays, with machinery everywhere, to start making them by hand ; and even if I did start without a machine, how can I buy a horse and the horse-gear for turning—and mother to keep too ? " he added. " Tell you what, Trixy," he blurted out, " you ain't content to be a woodman's wife, are you ? That's it, ain't it ? "

" Oh, Martin ! " she protested.

" If you ain't content to be a woodman's wife," Martin continued, " we might raise enough money to go to the colonies and keep mother going—and your dad's getting past work. We might try the colonies. I ain't so struck with Canada myself, but New Zealand now is the country where a working man is allowed to be a man and not only a servant."

" There is nothing demeaning in being a servant to the *real* gentry," said Trixy haughtily. " New Zealand is so far away, and I know her ladyship will, if you would but take it, find you a place as gamekeeper, or perhaps a bailiff in time."

" Oh ! " groaned Martin, overwrought with the thought of being so misunderstood by his sweetheart. " Do you think I would go round with those cockney fools with a gun, lick their boots for a tip, or spend my days touching my cap ? "

" How can you speak so about a most respectable calling, Martin ! "

" Why, it makes me downright sick. Look at those overfed hogs standing about inside and outside Tanhurst. I want to work for my living and be independent, and you know that, Trixy."

Trixy shot one more shaft, and it was tipped with irony.

" How can you be independent on about a pound a week ? "

Martin was speechless. Trixy, heated by the controversy with her lover, rose to go. He was evidently hopeless. He would never get on. Well, she had done her duty. She had tried to make him see how he might prosper if he would but choose to follow her directions. But he was an obstinate man. Yes, that was what was wrong about Martin : he was obstinate. She could hardly resist one abusive epithet.

" You are a rank——" and then she hesitated. Her ladyship used the expression. Pouting her lips, Trixy rushed out of the hut.

Martin with heavy hands took up a hazel wand and held it over the fire. When he looked round again he saw the timber-merchant walking down a cleared drive with

Trixy—walking within the purple walls of his beloved underwood.

Three months later old Ned Lipscombe came up to Martin in the woods, walking with an awkward gait, and a dour expression on his face.

" 'Eard the news, Martin, matey ? " he said tenderly to his young companion of the woods, who was lustily felling an oak tree with a long-handled axe. The sap of life was now running riot in every limb of the tree. Martin stopped to listen for a moment with uplifted axe.

" Young monkey Tim 'as got 'er—dam him and his pieces ! Gran' weddin' soon. You don't ketch Trixy makin' no backdoor marriage. She makes no error. Never you mind, matey ; she's got so far up the 'ill now, there's no ketching 'er up."

Martin looked dazed for a moment. High overhead a flock of wild geese flew by over the clearing. He buried his rough, toil-smitten knuckles in the sockets of his eyes, which, blazing with wrath, looked towards Tanhurst Place, standing behind the distant, lofty rookery, black and dominant.

" That's what done it ! " he cried, flourishing his great axe towards the Big House. " It ruins its maid-servants and its men-servants inside and outside—curse it ! "

A gleam of red light seen through the tracery of the bare branches, now burgeoning into new life, shot across the sky. It ran with the colour of blood along the gleaming edge of the axe which Martin struck with fierce incision into the heart of the oak. Shrieking, it fell with a crash to the ground.

CHAPTER IV

A TRILOGY

Before an Enquiry

A petition signed by at least four householders of any rural district, if sent to the Local Government Board, may, in the event of the District Council not acting, bring about an Enquiry (*vide* Housing and Town Planning Act, 1909).

WINTERBORNE STICKLAND lies under the shadow of a big house. One cannot help thinking of Thomas Hardy. It savours of Wessex tales. Lying in the deep folds of the hills, under ancient thatched roofs, tipped here and there with green moss, it lends itself to romance, and also lends itself to that pessimism which saturates the literature of Dorsetshire. Its lord lives at Milton Abbey, and at this beautiful and historic seat he entertained the late King Edward. His name is Sir Everard Hambro, and he is one of the wealthiest members of our plutocracy. He is not a landowner struggling to keep up appearances on a rent-roll derivable from poor farms and decaying cottages. He is a banker.

Mr. Lloyd George's land tax strikes little fear into the heart of the rich man who piles up his great wealth beyond the reach of those whose eyes are cast only on the soil. He is not in the unfortunate position of the land-owner, the owner of 5,000 acres who complained to me with real regret that he could not afford even to re-thatch the roofs of many of his cottages. Sir Everard Hambro is the entertainer of kings.

For the last forty years village affairs have apparently gone on with little to disturb the placidity of its quiet progress. The villagers took every advantage that they could of the Parish Council Act, even to the extent of providing the parish with a system of public lighting, an excellent water-supply, and a large acreage of allotments. The village prospered as far as its inhabitants, as a race divorced from the soil, could make it prosper. But in forty years children become fathers and mothers of sons and daughters who in the natural course of things marry and give birth to their children. In forty years the old cottages become unpleasantly crowded.

As the Rural Magna Charta had not in the least helped these villagers to get new and clean cottages, the Parish Councillors made

first of all an appeal to the lord of the soil, Sir
Everard Hambro.   Then in May of last year
they appealed to the Rural District Council
to adopt the Housing Act.   In August the
Medical Officer of Health reported that "the
condition of many cottages was obviously
conducive neither to health nor yet morality."

Let us look into some of these cottages as
seen by the eyes of the Special Correspondent
of the *Daily News*, the only daily paper
which troubled to report this drama of village
life, fatal though its ending might be to the
interests of the nation.

Cottage 1.—Father, mother, two grown-up
daughters, two grown-up sons, and a boy of 10
sleep in two tiny rooms.

Cottage 2.—Father, mother, and five children
sleep in two tiny rooms.   Fever has now broken
out here.

Cottage 3.—Father, mother, grandmother, two
sons aged 16 and 10, and one daughter aged 14,
sleep in two rooms.

Cottage 4.—Father, mother, three grown-up sons,
and a daughter aged 24, sleep in two rooms.

Cottage 5.—Father, mother, and two grown-up
sons sleep in one room.   Until recently there were
three sons at home.

Cottage 6.—Father, mother, and three children
sleep in one room not much larger than a big cupboard.

Further, this correspondent reports on two
cottages :

One was originally a stable or part of a stable.
The only place for keeping food is four feet below
the level of the immediately adjoining churchyard,
the damp from the soil of which penetrates the wall.
The two " bedrooms " in the stable loft are in
almost total darkness. The stable is occupied by
a widow, her son of 18, her daughter of 15, and a
lodger ; and the rent is 2s. a week.

In the second case, half a converted barn was
occupied by a Parish Councillor, his wife, two
grown-up sons, and a grown-up daughter, sleeping
in two miserably inadequate bedrooms. The hovel
is in a shocking state of repair. The rent is 1s. 9d.
a week.

One would naturally suppose that on the
publication of the Medical Officer's report
a warm-hearted, wealthy landlord would have
exclaimed, " I was quite ignorant of this state
of things, and adequate cottage accommodation must be found for all these poor people
immediately " ; that a proud man who lived
up to the motto of " Noblesse oblige " would
say to his agent, " Every person on my land
must be properly housed." But Sir Everard
Hambro had other views, and he was loyally
supported by his vicar, who received a stipend
for preaching the gospel of Christ. Immediately after the publication of the report Sir
Everard issued through his agent notices to
quit to six of his tenants, including the vice-
chairman of the Parish Council, who had taken
an active part in petitioning for more cottage

accommodation, and in December the chairman of the Parish Council also received notice to quit.

Meanwhile Sir Everard, in a letter written last September to the chairman of the Rural District Council, gave expression to his views on the matter :

My attention having been called to the matter (of the dearth of houses), I looked into it and came to the conclusion that if I gradually got rid of those who did not work in the parish there would be plenty of room for those who did. Until the Medical Officer's visit the other day, I did not like to give the notices, for I knew that though there was a little overcrowding in Stickland I thought if I sent away those who worked in another parish they would find even less accommodation there than in Stickland. I hope that, now I have taken the necessary steps to get rid of the others, the accommodation will be sufficient for those who remain, and that it will not be found necessary to build more cottages, except perhaps one or two on the farms.

Except perhaps one or two on the farms. The farmers who sit on the Council should be placated.

The beautiful sentiments expressed in this letter as to getting rid of honest, hard-working people and admittedly pitching them into other parishes just as overcrowded as Stickland, received the approval of the chairman

of the Rural District Council, who was also
in receipt of a stipend for preaching the gospel
of Christ—the Rev. F. Salmon, the vicar of
Langton Long.

Sir Everard went further. In carrying out
the mediæval policy of. " decanting," he
narrowed down those who were permitted to
stay to those actually employed on the estate ;
for on September 12 his agent writes to Mr.
Frederick Elford, who had lived in Stickland for fifty years, a notice to quit, of which
the preamble runs thus :

SIR,—The local authorities have complained of
the overcrowding which now exists at Stickland.
In order to reduce this overcrowding we find it
is necessary to acquire the cottages of the tenants
who are not actually employed on the estate.

Then came the notice to the chairman of
the Parish Council :

SIR,—In view of the wishes of the Parish Council
that cottages should be let to suit the wants of
families, it has been considered best that all cottages
should be let on weekly tenancies.

It was natural enough that the fear of
losing their homes, which means often not only
loss of occupation but the heavy expenses
of removal and the loss of garden crops,

9

struck terror into the hearts of Dorset folk
who had lived so long under the shadow of a
great house. Nevertheless a few held manfully to their citadels. An adverse Rural
District Council and a dictatorial overlord
did not deter them from requesting the
Local Government Board to hold an Enquiry
under the 1909 Housing and Town Planning
Act.

The people waited patiently and in great
hopes for the movement of that lever that
would lift the load of anxiety and oppression
from their minds and their bodies. But the
great engineer of Whitehall who fashioned the
lever made no forward movement with his
hand. In the meantime the rearrangement
of tenants went on. Old-age pensioners of
74 and 75, and another couple of over 80
who had lived for sixty years in one house,
were removed from homes in which were
enshrined the most sacred associations of their
lives. Eventually, the Battersea democrat
sent an inspector down only. But he held a
" private enquiry " and witnessed, apparently
with satisfaction, the housing problem solving
itself by the cunning method of " decanting."
He returned to Whitehall apparently with a
promise from Sir Everard Hambro to build
four more cottages.

Sir Everard has now bought up the only

piece of freehold property where an evicted
tenant might find permanent refuge, and that
is rented by Mr. Gillingham, who is under
notice to quit. Sir Everard is not a proud
man, though an entertainer of kings and a
game-preserver on a princely scale.

This modest man's father was a Dane.
It is hard to think that rich foreigners can
come to England, purchase a large tract of our
countryside, and become a lord of the soil
to whom our fellow-men, with the blood
of Saxon chieftains in their veins, should
have to bow the knee as a subject race.
But though it is not a far cry from Copen-
hagen to Lombard Street, neither is it many
leagues from Winterborne Stickland to Foxham, where live lords of the soil in whose
veins runs the blood of our oldest English
aristocracy.

It is true that the notices to quit—except
that to Mr. Gillingham—have, at the time I
write, the 26th of October, been withdrawn;
but the people are not to have control of
these four new cottages. They will be owned
by Sir Everard Hambro, and he will control
the lives of those who live in them, and the
two men who have borne the brunt of the
battle are face to face with the possibility of
meeting the fate of most reformers. Mr.
Gillingham, the chairman of the Parish

Council, has occupied his cottage for forty-eight years. Mrs. Kingsbury was born in the cottage where she has lived with her husband for the past forty years. Should they be driven from the parish in which they have lived all their lives, the labourers of Dorset will once more ask, " What is the good of Rural Magna Chartas ? What is the good of your Housing Acts, when, in the face of tragic revelations such as these, Acts of Parliament are powerless to free us from the tyranny of private ownership ? "

At an Enquiry

The story begins in October 1910, when Mr. James Mead, a house-painter by trade and a member of the Parish Council, raised the subject of the bad conditions of housing in his village. He proposed that the Parish Council should address a complaint to the Devizes Rural District Council. But his own Parish Council consisted almost entirely of land-owners, land-agents, tradesmen, and farmers, including amongst their number the two Rural District Councillors for the parish. He found only one supporter, and that was a fellow-workman. Undeterred, he organised a petition from the parishioners to the Parish Council.

Though many of the occupants of overcrowded cottages were afraid to sign the
petition, fearing eviction or being on bad terms
with their landlords in the matter of repairs,
he actually obtained twenty-four signatures.
The petition, however, produced no effect.
Then, at the election in March 1911, an attempt
was made to oust Mr. Mead from his seat on
the Parish Council. But this village Hampden
tenaciously held his own, and in January
1912, with insistent urgency, he proposed
that the Parish Council should call the attention of the Rural District Council to the
unsatisfactory condition of the cottages in
Potterne. He was instantly met with a flat
refusal by his own Council. Indeed, more
than a flat refusal: the chairman gratuitously
informed him that if the resolution were
forwarded to the Rural District Council it
would be "shown the door almost before it
got in."

Driven against the wall, there was nothing
for it now but to appeal to headquarters for
help—that is, to the Local Government Board.
The Rev. W. H. Hewlett Cooper, rector of
Tockenham, near Wootton Bassett, visited
the scene on behalf of the National Land
and Home League, and inspired the men with
hope at the time when they were almost in
the depths of despair.

Under Mr. Cooper's supervision a document was drawn up and signed by Mr. Mead and five of the boldest of his friends. The drawing up of this document is a very important affair in the lives of these villagers. Mr. John Burns will not look at a petition unless the technical phrasing of the document is absolutely correct. This seems to be a tradition of the bureaucratic department of the Government over which he has assumed a dictatorship. This is where the National Land and Home League can come to the aid of the humblest of country folk.

The issue became dramatic. There seemed no flaw in the document, nothing for the bureaucratic mind to quibble over. The appeal was made on March 9, 1912. Mr. John Burns, with an unusual promptitude for a chief of a circumlocution office, wrote to the Rural District Council on March 21, inviting its comments. The Council duly made them ; but their defence of a policy of alert inactivity did not sufficiently impress itself upon Mr. John Burns, and on May 10 the following official notice was posted all over the district :

THE HOUSING OF THE WORKING CLASSES ACTS,
1890 to 1909.

RURAL DISTRICT OF DEVIZES.
PARISH OF POTTERNE.

WHEREAS complaint has been made to the Local Government Board under Section 10 of the Housing, Town Planning, etc., Act, 1909, by four inhabitant householders of the Rural District of Devizes in the County of Wilts, that the Rural District Council of Devizes have failed to exercise their powers under Part III. of the Housing of the Working Classes Act, 1890, in regard to the provision of accommodation for the housing of the working classes in the parish of Potterne in a case where those powers ought to have been exercised :

AND WHEREAS the Local Government Board have, in pursuance of the said enactment, directed a public local Enquiry to be held into the subject-matter of such complaint :

NOTICE IS HEREBY GIVEN that WILLIAM HENRY COLLIN, Esquire, the Inspector appointed to hold the said Enquiry, will attend for that purpose at the National Schools, Potterne, on Thursday, the Twenty-third day of May, 1912, at Six o'clock in the Evening, and will then and there be prepared to receive the evidence of any persons interested in the matter of the Enquiry.

Local Government Board,   H. C. MONRO,
    10th May, 1912.   *Secretary.*

Then began much fluttering in the dovecots. The reign of self-complacency and stubborn indifference was over. Stagnant parochial officialism was stirred to its muddy depths, and owners began to get agitated. Mead, at the Parish Council meeting previous to the enquiry, was heckled and browbeaten. Owners of property, even those who were magistrates, took the undignified course of rushing round to the overcrowded cottages and warning the tenants about rents being raised, cowing them into silence with stories of people being turned out on to the roadside and the likely fate of Mead, who had been publicly heckled and "printed out in the newspapers." This mean form of intimidation is apparently not punishable under the Corrupt Practices Act, and yet it is a kind of undue influence far more common than that which takes place at election times. It produced the desired effect, and intimidation did not stop here. The whole stage-management of the Enquiry itself produced its chilling effect upon a scared village populace.

The front benches were occupied by the chairman of the Parish Council, Mr. Medlicott, a land-agent. By him sat Mr. W. Stancomb, the largest landowner in the parish. Just behind him sat the vicar, accompanied by Mrs. Medlicott and two other resident ladies. The third bench was occupied by large farmers. Two of the ladies made no concealment of their partisanship, applauding any evidence speciously put forward to show that cottages were not needed, and when a statement was read concerning Mr. Mead's repeated baffled attempts to obtain justice, they turned ostentatiously to the farmers sitting behind them to enjoy for one brief moment an account of Mr. Mead's discomfiture. Then, when a solicitor engaged by the National Land and Home League went through the painful list of overcrowded cottages—so many to the house, so many to the room, so many to the bed, they appeared to regard the matter, wrote Mr. Charles Roden Buxton, who was present, as a good joke.

It is inconceivable that gentlewomen could behave like this ; and I am sorry to have to record that this evil, stifling atmosphere, pro-jected by the landlord-employer class, had the effect of a drug on the minds of the labourers ; though, to the honour of the working women, up to the last they urged their men to come forward.

The chief witnesses from amongst the labouring poor had to pass up from the back of the long, narrow room, past the front benches, and then to stand facing the front benches, on which sat their landlords and employers. Under the very eyes of land-lords and employers had they to make their indictment. The result was what might have been expected. Few cared to face the music. Only two men had the courage to give evidence, the two village Hampdens, Mead and Underwood. When a third was called a response from the back of the hall came, " I'm going to have no voice in it." It was futile to summon more ! Armed with the bitter logic of facts the solicitor of the National Land and Home League indicted the Rural Councillors. With legal precision he read aloud that "Black List " the details of which roused the risibility of the ladies of culture :

Husband and wife and five children, whose ages range from 9 to 28 years, living in a house with two bedrooms only.

Husband and wife and four children, all over 14 years—two bedrooms.

Husband, wife, and five children, 21 to 38 years, (four sons and one daughter)—two bedrooms.

Husband and wife and seven children, 7 to 12, and grandmother—two bedrooms.

Husband, wife, and four children, 1½ to 13—one bedroom.

Husband, wife, and three children, 7 to 19—one bedroom.

Husband, wife, and three children, 2 to 7—one bedroom.

Widower, two sons, 17 and 20, three daughters, 9, 11, and 13—two bedrooms.

Husband, wife, and five children, from 10 downwards—two bedrooms.

Two families (two husbands and wives) and a lodger—two bedrooms.

Husband, wife, and five children, 1 to 16—two bedrooms.

Husband, wife, and four children, 1 to 17—two bedrooms.

Husband, wife, and seven children, 2 to 14—two bedrooms.

Husband, wife, and eight children, 2 to 18—two bedrooms.

Husband, wife, and six children, 1 to 13—two bedrooms.

Husband, wife, and seven children, 2 to 15—two bedrooms.

Husband, wife, and six children, 2 to 13—two bedrooms.

Husband, wife, and seven children, 1 to 10—the wife's father and sometimes another relative—two bedrooms.

Husband and wife, and seven children, 1 to 15—two bedrooms.

Now, the extraordinary thing was, not a single official nor landowner disputed the accuracy of this plain but grave arraignment of the exalted ones, so carefully had the League prepared the statements. On the contrary, the evidence of the District Medical Inspector and the local Sanitary Inspector only added to its force. Indeed, the Sanitary Inspector, who minutely inspected the Potterne houses before the Enquiry, said that half the houses had less than 300 cubic feet per person, whilst some had under 200 cubic feet per person ; and yet 300 cubic feet per person, as the County Medical Officer pointed out, was the minimum air-space permitted in a common lodging-house.

The official excuse for inaction was based

on a tale of averages, a useful document, no doubt, for the archives of Devizes, but one totally inadequate for the purpose of showing the true state of affairs. These averages displayed the innocuous-looking figures of 3'6 persons per house in the parish. An average of 3'6 may be quite satisfactory to the official mind, but to the simple mind who is one of seven or eight other simple minds sleeping in two bedrooms, the fact that there is only a married couple, or possibly no one, in the next cottage has but little interest. It appeared that there were ten empty cottages, but seven of these were shown to be uninhabitable, and when an advertisement for one of the other remaining three was read in court—

To let. Crown Place, Potterne, small cottage and garden, suitable for married couple with no family—

the case for void cottages fell through. "No family" was instructive.

Frantic efforts were made before the Enquiry came on to remedy congestion by forcing parents to put out some of their children to sleep in other cottages, and for the benefit of those (like the ladies of Potterne) whose imagination cannot see anything tragic in the bald statements in the "Black List" I append the following paragraph, taken from the *Daily Chronicle*, May 24, 1912 :

I visited several of the cottages in question, and found some very striking facts. There have been a score of cottages pulled down or vacated during the last few years, and none have been rebuilt. Modern sanitary accommodation is lacking in nearly all the cottages, the " bucket " system being in use, and one set of four cottages have to make use of one closet. Diphtheria has been prevalent, and a few years ago thirty children died in a few weeks ; they were buried in what is now known as " Angel Corner" in the churchyard. . . . A ceiling in one house fell through on to the bed. In one house was a well, covered over, in the front room, and in another ivy was growing inside the house, and had to be cut out at intervals. Some of the walls were almost stripped of paper, which was caused by the mildew in the winter. In two bedrooms above slept a man, his wife, and a young man lodger, their married daughter, her husband and one child. . . . Some of the tenants have rigged out a bed of a sort in the pantry, and one woman informed me, who had been summoned to " abate the nuisance" of overcrowding, that her children " were not nuisances, even if two of them did have to go out to another house to sleep." I noticed that some of the dwellings had hardly any back at all, and for a country place this is very unusual, but the cottager tends to his garden in front, and trailing creepers, homely flowers, and honeysuckle strove to hide some of the ugliness which a keen inspection reveals.

And yet this is the picturesque Wiltshire village which boasts of the old Elizabethan

Porch House of which you may see a repro-
duction in Shakespeare's England.

The upshot of it all is, the village Hampdens
have won their victory.   Mr. John Burns, in
the face of the appalling evidence, was compelled to issue the necessary order to the
Rural District Council.*   But it is a labourer's
victory won at the usual cost—the persecu-
tion and boycotting of the principal reformers.
Those who have conspired against the national
health can still do incalculable damage.   And
it is not only those who take an active part
who have to suffer.   There is a general up-
heaval in village life, in which petty tyranny
is exercised over some of the weakest and most
innocent.   I heard, for instance, of a girl in a
neighbouring village who had to endure the
penalty for " making herself busy."   She was
a young servant, who, being at home for a
week's holiday, spoke rather strongly in her
village about the condition of her parents'
cottage.   A short time afterwards a lady
called on the servant's mistress and asked
her if she was aware that one of her maids

---

* Since the above lines were written, the Rural District
Council has been ordered to get twelve new cottages built
and seventy old ones made habitable: 4s. 6d. and 5s. are
said to be the rents for new cottages—rents beyond the
means of the agricultural labourer.   But for once the
Local Government Board has insisted upon cottages being
built, *whether there is to be a charge on the ratepayers or not.*

spent her holiday in an overcrowded cottage, and was it not too bad of servants to spend their holidays in this way and then to return to their places and "mix with our dear children "? This humane informant and subtle adviser was the wife of the man who owned the cottage in question. The result was the maid received notice to go, in spite of the fact that her mistress knew very well how many brothers and sisters she had at home, and had sometimes joked about it, for it was not the first time that the girl had slept at home. But she had committed the unpardonable social sin of mentioning that overcrowding existed.

As a parson friend of mine remarked, " The administration of the Housing Acts seems to have stimulated the Máchiavellian ingenuity of ' the gentry ' at the present time."

It has been, as I have said, a labourer's victory. But suppose that there had been no powerful organisation like the National Land and Home League behind these six men of Potterne ; suppose there had been no friendly parson from a neighbouring village to draw up a case ; suppose no lawyer had been engaged, and that there were no kindly subscribers behind these men subject to a week's notice and in danger of losing their jobs—what then ? Fear, no doubt, would have chilled the heart of the bravest of the reformers, as it very nearly did at the Enquiry, leaving two men alone to fight the battle of the people. Potterne would become another derelict English village, in which human lives would be sacrificed before the Golden Calf.

After an Enquiry

Wiltshire, like Dorsetshire, is a county of great estates over which the landlord's agent and the farmer have long ruled with an iron hand. Two of the largest estates in the county are owned by two prominent politicians, Lord Lansdowne and Mr. Walter Long, and both of these gentlemen have stated publicly that they are in favour of some kind of rural programme to stay the exodus to the town. It is full time that they promulgated a reform for the English peasant, who in these counties is the worst paid and the worst housed in Europe.

In the light of Lord Lansdowne's speech before the Rural League on July 24, 1912, the story of the evictions at Foxham in January of this year make curious reading. Lord Lansdowne now favours the building of cottages by public authority. It was a great pity he did not stir up his agent and his tenant-farmers to bring this about on his own estate a year ago.

Last year Lord Lansdowne offered for sale 1,000 acres in the hamlet of Foxham. Owing to the demand for small holdings the County Council (generally adverse to administering the Small Holdings Act) bought 193 acres, and on this farm eight families received notice to quit. Some of the other cottages were bought by farmers who wanted them for their own employees, and so they, too, got rid of the occupying tenants. Of the forty-seven cottages in Foxham, thirty-five changed hands, and when once a man leaves a cottage in a district like this, he generally has to go in search of other employment. Overcrowding existed at the time of the sale of the property. Now it meant folk actually being turned out on to the roadside.

The Parish Council—typically Wiltshire—consisted of seven farmers and two labourers. They made no move to get cottages built. But the two labourers, armed with Mr. John Burns's Town Planning Act, sent an application of their own, signed also by two other men, for the application of the Housing Act to the Rural District Council at Calne. Calne is the centre of the pig industry, and its Rural District Councillors, it is recorded, received the application with swinish laughter. With a chuckle of sardonic merriment they referred the matter to the Parish Council

10

of Bremhill—the Parish Council on which seven of their farmer friends sat. An application was also sent to the County Council.

No response save a curt acknowledgment came from the County Council to these poor labourers of Foxham in direful distress. " The Cerberus of officialism had snarled them back with all his three pairs of jaws," wrote Lieut.-Col. D. C. Pedder, who lives in this neighbourhood. The appeal then had to go to headquarters—that is, direct to the President of the Local Government Board. Through the good offices of the National Land and Home League there was sufficient *prima facie* evidence for Mr. John Burns to order an immediate Enquiry. This time twenty men came forward in the crowded little village schoolroom to bear witness as to the lack of cottages, and how, under notice to quit, they had searched in vain for a house. The tragedy of one man, with seven children down with whooping cough, under notice to quit an overcrowded cottage, was startlingly revealed, and the story of how the youths and girls were driven to the towns was unfolded.

But all that the Enquiry produced for these people was a vengeful retaliation on the part of the recalcitrant councillors.

What happened was an eviction as brutal

as any in the annals of English country life. The County Council, one of the three jaws of the three-mouthed Cerberus, promptly took its revenge. It snapped at the two ringleaders and threw their bodies out upon the roadside.

Had this happened in Ireland, under a Tory Administration, the Liberal press would have rung with the horrors of it; but as it happened in a Wiltshire village hamlet, the only report of it is that which appeared in the *Wiltshire Advertiser*, written by Mr. Montague Fordham, who was an eye-witness of the scene:

On Friday, January 21, an extraordinary step was taken at Avon, a hamlet of Foxham, in the eviction of two men, Robert Grimshaw and Alfred Fortune, two members of the Land and Home League, from the cottages where they had lived for many years.

Some half-dozen policemen under the direction of the officials carried out the work. They gave no word of warning to the tenants; but when they arrived there was no delay. Everything was promptly cleared out and heaped in the deep snow. The kettles were lifted off the hobs, the " taters " that were cooking for dinner were taken; the fires were put out; the hearths were made desolate.

It was afternoon when I arrived, delayed in part by the flooded road. " Where is the rector of Tockenham ? " was the question put to me at once, as I jumped out of the motor. " He is not well, and unable to come : we were taken by surprise," I said. There was a look of sorrow and disappointment in the group that surrounded me, for the rector is greatly beloved here ; he has been the leader and friend of the people, and his help and sympathy were needed.

I turned from my questioner to look at the scene. The red sun was sinking behind dark ricks, their tops whitened with snow, and fringed with a hundred icicles ; the air was full of grey mist, and in it stood the crowd, some crying, some laughing hysterically, but most silent—as country people are when faced by a tragedy far too common in country life.

And behind the little crowd, in front of two cottages, were the belongings of the tenants, an indescribable mass on the roadside. There was the bedding, damp already ; the furniture ; the odds-and-ends of all sorts ; the geraniums from the cottage windows, dying in the cold ; the little ornaments that had decked the parlours ; the children's toys ; everything which went to make the home. By it stood the two evicted men—Bob Grimshaw, justly angry and somewhat excited ; his neighbour, Alfred Fortune, calmer and silent— each with a family of children—quite little children. A woman was crying in a pitiful undertone, and a little lad kept breaking into sobs.

It is not surprising that Wiltshire people are greatly stirred by this tragedy, so near to the lives of all. Never, perhaps, since the days of Joseph Arch has there been such excitement.

It may be argued, But what alternative had the County Council, if the men would not quit the cottages, to let in the new tenants? The County Council *had* an alternative, and that is where its callousness was evinced. It

Photo] *[Porter, Chippenham.*

"After an Inquiry"—the Eviction at Foxham, Wilts. The evicted families are seen here, but the cottages are not visible.

To face page 148.

could, had it chosen, have provided cottages with an acre of land attached, to every one of the displaced families which had been under notice to quit. This it could easily have done under a provision of the Small Holdings Act of 1908. But the County Council did not even wait for the result of the Enquiry. Its action was inexcusable. It struck swiftly with intent to injure.

Some very extraordinary evidence was brought out at the Enquiry. Lord Lansdowne's agent actually said he had never known that there was any demand for cottages at Foxham. The surveyor of the district " had never heard of any demand for cottages." The chairman of the Rural District Council, which is held at the centre of the pig industry, had never " heard of a want of housing accommodation in that parish." The men who took a leading part in the Enquiry have now been driven out of the neighbourhood.

No wonder the village labourer feels that the odds are too much against him for a fair fight for justice. In his hazard of life he has to play with those who have loaded dice. If he wins, the cost of victory is too heavy for him to pay. And has he much hope of a more generous treatment by the Imperial Government ?—that one hope still left to him.

It may be that at the present moment he is hearing the guns at Portsmouth and filled with a sickening fear that, from a hundred guns of Churchill's great fleet, the Chancellor's thousand new cottage homes may be blown into smoke.

CHAPTER V

THE GREAT ESTATE

THE pessimism of Thomas Hardy seems deeply rooted in the soil of Dorset. We know that in the fine, sensitive veins of Richard Jefferies there flowed a strong current of pessimism, in spite of all his strenuous efforts to present a brave face to the world by finding joy in the flora and fauna around the great estates of Wessex. He brushed aside all consideration of writing of the human fauna as long as he could. Sprung from the yeoman class himself, it was difficult for him to sympathise with those whom his class traditionally treated as servants. But before his end came, the bitterness of the lives of those who toiled for others without adequate reward seared the great heart of Jefferies and evoked from him a series of imperishable prose poems.

Cobbett, Jefferies, Hardy, and Hudson never seem to have penetrated into the heart of Wessex without experiencing a touch of its desolating blight. Mr. W. H. Hudson, an aristocrat of letters in whose veins there runs a strong sympathy for the aristocracy of land, has, it is evident, felt too the tyranny of this countryside. He has shown us facets of it in the crystal prose of *Afoot in England* and *The Life of a Shepherd.*

Wessex is a country of great estates, and it is in Dorset that the great owners appear to make themselves most powerfully felt. In those misleading idylls of English country life written by townsmen, or by the countrymen who lead sequestered, scholarly lives, it has been the custom to show how pleasant are the lives of the cottagers living under a condition of benevolent despotism.

To say that landlords are inherently wicked, or worse than any other of the possessing classes, is, of course, absurd; but where they are kindly and exercise a benevolent despotism over their estates the effect is always disastrous to the manhood of our peasantry. It is the social system that is at fault, in vesting so much power in one individual. As a picture of village life under a benevolent despotism, a description written by a friend, the wife of a country parson, is illuminating :

The whole of this village is in the feudal ages still, though under a kindly overlord. New cottages are built as they are wanted, and old ones enlarged. It is true that everyone is better off than he would be as owner, but this prosperity is, in our eyes, very dearly bought indeed. Where the people are loyal by long tradition to the —— it is rather charming sometimes, but where they are not loyal, and just " keep in " with the powers-that-be, the degradation seems to us very great.

No tyranny is exercised here except that shillings are spent on persons who would much rather spend sixpence for themselves ; but the people who do look down upon the labourers and try to keep them " in their place " are the farmers.

The squire would not turn out an old woman, though she took up the house-room of a large family ; but the farmer would sweep everything before his wishes. Cottages were much wanted in Wiltshire, and I never could find out whose fault it was that they were not built. The squire (always absent) let the farms on condition that certain old people were not turned out, and the farmer (one man took all the farms) used to get men from the neighbouring workhouse, put them in huts in the summer, and sack them in the winter. The farmer and the landlord could not probably come to terms about the cottages, but the farmer's policy in the village was to get bad and cheap material in the matter of horses and men, knock the horses on the head at the end of the summer, leave their carcases in the fields, and send the men to the workhouse. He only kept a few shepherds, a skilled thatcher, and one or two others not easily replaced.

He openly objected to his men going to church, which seems as bad as one squire-parson in Sussex, who sacked everyone who went to chapel.

The absence of cottages led to the illegitimacy of several children, as the labourers considered that the marriage ceremony was of no account unless one went to one's own cottage.

Last year we walked in the forest of Thuringia, and thought the peasants were far poorer and worked far harder than our Dorset folk, but saw how much more satisfactory and manly was their independent life. This year we have been among the Basques of France and Spain. These people live on bread as hard as wood and as brown as the earth, washing it down with buttermilk, but yet are as princes in gaiety and the real food of life when compared to the sneaking, creeping, cowed existence of our labourers within a week of the workhouse. The rich cannot make the poor happy, but still less, it seems to me, does the tenant-farmer do it. To be master of one's own little domain, subject only to reasonable good behaviour, is what most human beings want. . . . I knew what it was those eight years, and I know what it is to live under the paternal care of a lovable landlord and patron, who treats one with kindness and almost reverence ; and I prefer the little plot of freedom.

Now here is a good landlord, who owns a vast estate ; yet we see that however well he may treat his own cottage tenants, the real executive power lies in the hands of the large farmer—a power which the landowner is quite unable to check. Then, though the picture may be true, in rural romances, of well-thatched cottages, of sun-bonneted women drawing pure water from deep wells, of cottage children well looked after by some Lady Bountiful, of drainage made perfect so that infectious diseases cannot easily spread to the Hall that stands in the middle of the spacious park : what about the more common picture—a picture not to be seen so much as to be felt by those who are the chief figures in it ? Let us glimpse at a few of these pictures taken from my Dorsetshire note-book :

Landowner A has, I learn, £5,000 a year and no children to help him to spend his income at college or elsewhere. On his estate lives one of his gardeners, to whom he pays the princely wage of 15s. a week with a cottage "thrown in." This cottage has two small bedrooms, the bedrooms being 9 ft. by 7 ft. and 8 ft. by 6 ft., in which sleep the father, mother, and five children. The water-supply is drawn from a well in the garden, but this well is close to the cesspool, and two of the children go down with diphtheria.

The water is analysed and is found to contain cesspool drainage. Thereupon, the gardener's wife asks the Medical Officer to insist upon the owner providing a proper water-supply.

The Medical Officer, however, cannot see his way to do this, which brings forth the remark from the woman, " He attends the family, so he won't do anything." These cottagers were now ordered to fetch water from the owner's house in future. The house is a quarter of a mile distant, and the mother, knowing that the children when thirsty are certain to drink washing-up water, and having neither the time nor the strength to carry buckets of water from the Big House, decides to leave the cottage, and her husband his job.

Now the prolonged illnesses from the impure water cost her £5, of which the employer paid £1, and expressed the pious hope that she had saved some money ! After this incident the employer, finding cottage tenants objected to remaining long in his insanitary cottages, stipulated on yearly agreements with his tenant-employees.

Landlord B is another owner of a large estate in Dorsetshire. His income amounts to £15,000 a year. He has seven motor cars, so that, apparently, there should never be any delay in running away from the sight of his insanitary cottages when they fret his nerves—if ever they do. Most of his cottages have stone floors standing below the level of the ground, and water has to be bailed out in wet weather when the water-meadows are flooded. Whole families here become crippled with rheumatism. No repairs are ever made until the walls or the roof actually subside ; and if complaints are made dismissal is immediate.

Then there is Landlord C, who is a Peer of the Realm. On his estate the cottages are often overcrowded and rife with tuberculosis. In

one of these cottages a girl aged 17 lies ill
with consumption at the present moment.
She is the eldest of eight children, of whom
five sleep in a room 9 ft. by 8 ft.   When the
agent was asked to find some better cottage
he remarked that he really could not see
his way to trouble his lordship about such a
matter.

I need not harrow the reader by giving more
individual instances.   Many of the cottages
existing in Wessex are simply death-traps and
not homes.

An agent for a Friendly Society told me
this year that out of thirteen deaths in their
branch last year, eight were due to consumption, and these were comparatively
young lives.   He attributes this largely to
the old thatched cottages, which, though
picturesque, are as a rule very unhealthy.   In
many cottages the space between the thatch
and the rafters is open for birds, mice, and
rats to get in and breed their young above the
plaster.   This has been going on for generations, ever since the old hovels were built.
When new thatch is put on it is laid over
the old, which is sometimes 200 years old.
A fine breeding-place this for the germs
of disease, which quickly find their way
into the lungs of the children reared in these
stifling rooms, with their slot-holes for

windows which often do not open, and where fireplaces are a luxury. The cracks between the old, moth-eaten floor-boards are often filled with the filth accumulated during several generations. In these places vermin are bred, and when the floors are scrubbed a stench immediately arises. Farm-tied cottages often have the full benefit of the manurial water, waste from washing-tubs and dairy utensils, draining away under the windows, covered though they may be with honeysuckle and roses. Cottages built in farmyards are, of course, most sub-ject to the drainage from pigsties, cow-sheds, and stables; and wells sunk within a few yards of such buildings are, naturally enough, full of death-dealing bacteria. Is it any wonder that the labourer considers that it is less poisonous to drink the ale at the beer-house than to drink the water in his well?

In a certain heathland district of Dorset-shire, some cottages have been built in the past by squatters on a three- or four-life tenure. These have now fallen into the hands of the Lord of the Manor, and as they were old and out of repair, he pulled them down. In spite of the fact that cottages are very scarce and that the clay-workers have daily to walk three miles to their occupation, starting at five in the morning in winter, trudging over rough and boggy heath-tracks, and returning at dark after an arduous day of toil, no cottages have been rebuilt by this Lord of the Manor. He has given no reason for not building, though it is possible that he prefers to see heads of game with brilliant plumage on the moor to children with golden locks. The men have petitioned him to allow them to rebuild the heath cottages at their own expense, stating that they are willing even to pay an increased ground-rent, and to keep the cottages in good repair. Some of them went so far as to offer to buy their heath-plots, but the agent doggedly refused to let or sell, or to allow any building whatever to be put up. I may mention that a cottage in which to rest their rheumatic limbs is all these clay-workers look forward to. The old-age pension is no use to them. At sixty they are physical wrecks, after a life spent in standing long hours in the water and labouring incessantly.

I wonder what Mr. Lloyd George or Mr. John Burns would have said if this had happened in Ireland. But the Irish peasant has vociferous representatives whose voices never fail to reach the ears of Cabinet Ministers. The voice of the English peasant is never heard in the House of Commons, and Cabinet

Ministers have a strange way of keeping their ears filled with the rumours of war, so that no internal strife is audible to them.

We know that, to the eye of many a landed proprietor looking out of the windows of his mansion, a cottage chimney in the foreground is an unseemly sight. His eye should be allowed to roam across landscape uninterrupted by signs of human life other than his own. Now though most landlords are arbitrary about external things, such as the keeping of swine, few exercise their lordship over the domestic arrangements inside a cottage. In Dorset, though, it is different.

Within the bounds of a great estate a fisherman and his wife lived in a secluded cottage for thirty years. Their means were very narrow. They were scrupulously clean, and what is called "respectable." Their cottage was entirely out of view of the Big House, and three miles away from its owner, and they ventured to take a lodger for the summer weeks.

"A very quiet nice gentleman he was, busy writing in the morning, and would go for a walk in the afternoon," said the woman to a friend of mine. "He liked the quiet, and was fond of our little garden, and he was coming again this year. His bit of money would have made all the difference

to us, for whilst we had him we never went
short.   But the landlord came down, and
said that never as long as we lived in his
cottage was we to take no one.   He spoke
terrible, and said we was making his house
a common lodgin'-house."

This last remark hurt the cottagers very
deeply, but a landed proprietor can hardly
be expected to choose his words when speaking to a cottage tenant.

The economic tyranny practised by great
landowners unfortunately engenders a spirit
of petty tyranny amongst the tenant-farmers,
and it is at their hands the labourer has to
suffer most.

The result of all this is the labourers have
lost faith in the Parish Councils Act, in the
Small Holdings Act, and in the Housing Acts.

"We've got a Parish Council now," remarked a labourer to me, "but are we any
freer ?   Is a Parish Council any good when
men are afraid to speak out ? "

He then told me of an incident in his parish
where land was to let to the farmers at 12s.
an acre, and yet some of this land sublet to
the labourers as garden allotments at 6d. a
lug (pole).   The Parish Council is composed
of farmers, one or two labourers, and the
parson.   A proposal was made that the Parish
Council should apply to the landlords for all

II

the existing allotments at the average rent of the rest of the land, and that it should be sublet to the tenantry at a reasonable rent. Two of the farmers on the Council were the persons charging the excessive rent, and two other councillors were labourers living in their tied cottages, and paying this high rent for allotments. One of the farmers looked keenly at his man, and then asked the proposer why he had brought this forward and who had complained to him.

The proposer was not going to incriminate the labourers, so said that he had brought it forward quite on his own account, and asked the farmer if he could deny the fact of letting land at 6*d*. a lug which he got for 12*s*. the acre, and why the land in the same field was charged so much more for when let to the labourers.

The farmer replied that the labourer had no wages to pay and that the farmer had ! He was then asked how much produce the labourer would get out of his allotment if he did not put his own labour into it. No answer was given, but all sorts of arguments were brought up against the proposal, quite as senseless as the one mentioned, and the proposition fell through as the men were afraid to say anything or to vote against their masters.

If he be a poor man, one who has to sell his labour to an employer, the Parish Councillor's efforts to reform abuses invariably meet with some act of tyranny. A Parish Councillor, for instance, gave some information about some threatened evictions. Thereupon the agent of a well-known nobleman called at the cottage of this man, who was a labourer, and said to him with brutal frankness :

" You won't be allowed to remain here any longer. I'll have you put out on to the roadside, if it comes to that."

And he fulfilled his threat. The labourer was driven out of his village ; but no historian records this act of social heroism.

In this desolate land two Parish Councillors who were workmen applied a year ago for small holdings. Immediately after this they received notice to quit. This act of intimidation had the desired effect, for this year no labourer dares to present himself for election on the Parish Council.

For the ordinary cottager to complain to the landlord, agent, or sanitary authority, is to court immediate eviction. In one village a woman complained to her landlord, who was a wealthy tradesman, of sanitary arrangements. The family were immediately turned out, on the pretext that the owner wished to repair the cottage. This was last year, and yet the landlord has done nothing to the cottage, though he has declared himself quite willing to let it " to a quiet person."

In another village, on a labourer complaining of the condition of his cottage to his landlord, this gentleman replied with telling sarcasm, " You had better have a brand-new £300 house put up for you! You can quit."

" Well," said the labourer, " I don't want my family to share a convenience with three other families, or to live where you can't keep the rats from getting at your food. It's because I complain, I suppose, I have got to leave ? "

The callous answer was, " You ought to know that a still tongue makes a wise head."

A recent case of petty tyranny exercised by a farmer came under my notice, where a man was told to leave the farm-tied cottage because he had declined to buy milk from the farm. The reason why he did not buy milk from the farmer's cows was that one of the cows was " consumptious," so the labourer declared.

There are many ways of getting rid of a man you do not like from a farm-tied cottage, and the following is a plan adopted by a Wessex farmer. He will get someone to complain to the sanitary authorities of the condition of the cottage, and the tenant is ordered to leave by the Sanitary Inspector in order " to abate the nuisance."

Occasionally, but very rarely, a farm labourer resists the notice to quit the cottage, and the farmer, failing to frighten his man, threatens to sack a relative of the labourer's from some post. This was actually carried into effect quite recently by a school committee of which the farmer was a member.

" If I hear any more of your complaining about your drains I will find another tenant for your cottage. You be a proper sort of fool to think I have no better use for my money than in laying it out on all this tomfoolery about insanitary cottages. Mind what I tell you! " Thus spake the landlord to a labourer who retired into his hovel to bring up his children in an atmosphere charged with tubercular germs.

Wessex, a country of great estates, never seems to have thrown off that heritage of tyranny which ran riot in the magistracy of the pre-Victorian period. Six agricultural labourers, in 1834, were arrested at Tolpuddle for the heinous crime of joining a trade union in order to improve their wretched conditions. Though the Martyr's Tree is pointed out as a monument of the savagery of the country gentlemen of England in transporting these men to Botany Bay, it is very doubtful whether the men of Wessex feel to-day that they breathe a much freer atmosphere.

Their villages lie remote from the centres of intellectual activity. They seem out of touch with the outside world; segregated from social solidarity. They do not fight for the citadels to be won by fighting; they simply retreat from their villages, and the slums of the town become the inevitable counterpart of the solitude of the country. Everywhere across their sunlit pastures is cast the shadow of the Big House.

A case of vindictive tyranny was told me by a village schoolmaster concerning a labourer who was very much respected in his village, and became elected chairman of the Parish Council. By working very hard, and after much opposition, this chairman managed to get his Council to acquire 13 acres of land compulsorily for allotments. It happened that $8\frac{1}{2}$ of these 13 acres belonged to a farmer who farmed over 2,000 acres and was continually buying all the land on which he could lay his hands. Being wrathful at losing these $8\frac{1}{2}$ acres, he told a neighbour that he would drive the chairman of the Council out of the parish. He set about doing this in the usual way. He got hold of the old woman who owned the cottage in which the labourer lived, and made her a good offer for it. The old lady was surprised at the offer, but as her tenant had paid his rent regularly for many years she told him of the offer she had received. The labourer divined at once who had tried to buy the roof over his head. He spoke to his friends about it and they helped him to raise the price offered by his enemy for the cottage, and the landlady, sympathising with her tenant, sold it to him. The farmer was thwarted in his evil design, it is true; but nevertheless his action had the effect, upon a race already cowed by oppression, of checking the ardour of village Hampdens.

CHAPTER VI

THE LUST OF SPORT

The Fox and the Hen

To the farmer who does not ride to hounds, the sight of two score of crimson-coated men churning up the meadow turf laid down for hay, or ploughing up the seeds with their hoofs, without as much as " by your leave," and leaving gates flung open, must make him feel himself one of a conquered race, living under the heels of the conquerors, who are sure of meeting no resistance.

That farmers, who are parochially a very powerful race, have rarely attempted to prevent by law the Hunt riding over their fields willy-nilly, or to obtain legal protection against the depredations of the fox, which is an animal now bred purely for the pleasure of those who hunt, lends colour to my contention that there is a special tyranny of the countryside exercised by the lords of the soil whch no body of burgesses of any town in England would endure for a year without legislation.

I know that a number of well-to-do farmers ride to hounds, and that they are loud in their praises at the Rent dinner of the Master of the Hounds and his friends. The M.F.H. will respond by telling how the Duke of Wellington attached so much value to the hunting-field as a training-ground for his officers that he maintained a pack of hounds in the Peninsula during his six years' campaign against armies vastly superior in numbers to his own. Indeed, as a noble Earl said recently, where would the British Empire be to-day without fox-hunting ?

Farmers will listen to all this with eyes cast down after a good dinner. But they know very well that someone is pulling their leg ; they know very well that a pat on the back with a gloved hand and an invitation to an eighteen-penny lunch (or a " Come over in my motor and have some lunch there ") is hardly sufficient compensation—however pleasant they may feel the thrill of being comrades in the saddle with their betters—for broken fences, poached turf, injured plants of corn, and the loss of poultry, or for whole days spent looking for stock lost through the gates being left open.

Landlords who ride to hounds, or who subscribe to the Hunt because Algernon or Claude will soon come down from Oxford or Cambridge, deceive themselves if they think that the farmers who do not hunt put up with all this trespassing over their fields and wanton injury to their crops for pure love of the landed aristocracy. The servile spirit which is one of the evil heritages of feudalism still lives in the south-country farmer—a servile spirit which, born of the illicit union of lust and weakness, tramples on those weaker than itself.

But few farmers ever display the courage shown by Miss M. G. Cook, of the Stone Cross Poultry Farm, Ashurst, who in August 1912 issued this ultimatum :

REWARD. Having during the last two years had over 340 head of poultry killed by foxes, and not having received one penny compensation, we are now compelled to protect ourselves, and will give

5s. FOR EVERY FOX

delivered to us

DEAD or ALIVE !

" The West Kent Hunt have treated us disgracefully," she informed a *Daily News* interviewer. " We live here in the shadow of Ashurst Park, where the West Kent preserve foxes for their sport. During the six years our farm has been established we have lost roughly 300 pullets a year—all the depredation of foxes.

" We have always played the game straight, and we never claim compensation for the birds carried away. We confine our claims for those we find dead and mutilated on the farm. Our claims, which do not equal our losses by a very large margin, were paid by the Hunt up to 1910. Since then they have ignored us, and for my own protection I now have been bound to take extreme measures. Between last Monday and Friday twenty pullets—prize stock —were actually taken out of our wired-in pens in broad daylight.

" The members of the Hunt want good sport. They carefully preserve their foxes—and we supply the vermin with food for their ever-increasing families. That is too bad. We inform the Hunt every time we have losses, and we have continued to do so since 1910. No notice has been taken either by master or members, and all the consolation I have received has been a polite suggestion that I should move my farm to another place. The new M.F.H. recently wrote this to me :

" ' *I should advise you to go to some place where your present trouble would be impossible.*'

" Well, we gave the Hunt a time-limit up to last Saturday to decide if they would come to some satisfactory arrangement. They have done nothing, so we have taken the matter into our own hands, and when November comes they will be the sufferers.

" If the gentlemen who preach Tariff Reform were to act up to their belief and support those in their own village instead of rearing vermin to ruin a fellow-creature's living, we should then believe what they said was for the good of their country, and not for themselves ! It's a different kind of Protection that I'm seeking ! "

Some artificial earths have been made within a mile or two of my own holding, and cubs are constantly to be found on the farm next to mine, and so it is not to be wondered at that I have lost many a duck and many a hen. I have never hesitated to send in my claim promptly to the Hunt, nor ever failed to get a payment—that is, after I have had a preliminary brush with the gentleman to whom I have already referred, who takes politics as part of his winter sports. With the usual insolent gallantry of "the gentry" to a person living in a cottage, he began in my absence addressing my wife as, "Now, my good woman," but he left lifting his hat like a sulky schoolboy who has received a reproof. Against the staghounds I have openly declared war and have on more than one occasion had the satisfaction of giving the deer a good start of the hounds.

I remember one soft, muggy day in February, when looking over the hedge into my ten-acre hayfield—my one and only hayfield—I became suddenly conscious of a deer standing superbly erect, with quivering nostrils, quite close to me. It was hesitating whether to take the gate that led into the road or to attempt the high hedge, which would have landed it into my garden. Then almost instantaneously a number of redcoats, full of the lust of the chase, flashed across my vision. Suddenly the huntsman's horn was blown, the deer was sighted, and down from the upland farm forty gentlemen in pink came riding, riding straight for the fixed eve-gate that barred the way into my meadow.

The deer hesitated no longer : it made for the five-barred gate, leapt it with superb agility, and was off like the wind :

> So a fateful light lit up his eye,
>   And he opened his nostrils wide again,
> And he tossed his branching antlers high
>   As he headed the Hunt down the Chenlock glen,
>   As he raced down the echoing glen.
>   For five miles more, the stag, the stag,
>   For twenty miles, and five and five,
>   Not to be caught now, dead or alive,
>   The stag, the runnable stag.

Picking up a ten-foot pole, I ran as fast as I could, and, jumping the stream with it, reached the fixed eve-gate just as two men were smashing it down to let through the hounds. Sharply I told them that they were performing an act of wanton damage as well as of trespass, and brandishing my pole I defied the foremost riders to leap the hedge. I suppose they thought I meant business : indeed I did. After a passage of words, the colour of which was more riotously extravagant than the colour of their coats, the forty riders wheeled round, and I had the pleasure of hearing some of the prettiest oaths that have ever been uttered on a hunting-field. I had, too, the pleasure of listening to the heavy thuds of their horses' feet as they struck the muddy lane which bespattered their crimson coats. It was a long lane without a turning, and the deer had by now vanished into another county.

As it may be imagined, I am not *persona grata* with the Hunt. I do not receive invitations to lunch at the Annual Hunt Steeplechase. Not that there is any personal enmity between either the Master of the Foxhounds or the Master of the Staghounds and myself—for has not the Master of the Foxhounds taken tea with me after many a little " discussion " ?

On one occasion, when Master Reynard had taken several White Wyandotte hens, with the letter from the solicitors of the Hunt containing a cheque for the loss, I was coolly advised to keep my birds properly shut up at night. This advice is very much like one farmer saying to another, " I am going to turn my cattle into your fields, and it is your business to try and prevent them from getting in." One would have thought that a five-foot wire netting was sufficient to

keep out foxes.   Not a bit of it.   I lost
five White Orpingtons one night or early
morning through a fox clambering over the
netting and chasing the terrified hens.   For
these five pure-bred pullets, which in October
were worth quite 6s. each, I received a cheque
for 15s.

Now it is all very well for me, a peasant
proprietor, one who has nothing to sell to
those who ride to hounds, and possessing
a pen as my second line of defence against
the incursions of hordes of barbarians, to
have these little pleasantries with the Hunt.
But what of the small man who lives, as it
were, under the shadow of the Big House,
who rents his field from those who hunt
and those who shoot?

They know that to complain will mean,
very often, a refusal of necessary repairs
being done on the farm, or of a rebate of
rent in a bad season.

It is the small farmer, who cannot afford
to hunt, who has to suffer most, not only
from riders trespassing on his ground, but
also from the ravages of the fox amongst his
poultry, for it is the small farmer who invariably is the poultry-keeper of the neighbourhood.

I know a man who keeps poultry on a
farm of fifty acres.   He does not keep the

ordinary barn-door fowl which it is the tradition of the Hunt to regard as worth about half a crown. He makes his profits chiefly by selling sittings of day-old chicks and adult birds of pure breeds, and sometimes he pays as much as half a guinea for a cockerel when he introduces fresh blood into his pens. Now he told me the other day that he lost annually thirty or forty birds by the depredations of the fox. It is true he gets some compensation, but the compensation he receives never covers the value of his birds, to say nothing of the prospective profit if they are chickens of pure breed; and his losses do not stop here. He has now been obliged to give up keeping turkeys, for, as is well known, it is very difficult to house turkeys properly, and these often fall an easy prey at night to the fox. His living is made unnecessarily hard to win by his having to come down from his cottage a mile away to his farm every night to shut up his birds, which are scattered over fields and housed in innumerable coops and brooders. If you were to add up the labour he expends every year in performing this one act, the cash equivalent would come to a fairly large tax upon this man's industry.

" In the barn where we are standing," he said to me, " where you know I keep my fattening-pens, in spite of my dog being chained up inside here, a fox entered, and mangled no fewer than ten birds. Take notice of the dog? Why foxes round here are as tame as the hens."

" Why don't you complain more? " I said to him.

" What's the good? " he answered despondingly. " You know how I am fixed up under ——," and he pointed towards the direction of the Big House. " This country is a rich man's paradise, but it ain't no good doing anything but asking them to deal kindly by you."

It is not only a question of loss of birds, but also of the damage done to fields, for which compensation claims are very rarely pressed. Supposing the forty riders had come across my one meadow of ten acres shut up for hay. It was, as I have said, a damp, muggy day, and the turf was soft as a sponge after continuous rains ; moreover, the field had just been both rolled and harrowed. With a large farmer it is often only one or two of his many fields that are ridden over when following the hounds, and he shrugs his shoulders at the deeply imbedded hoof-marks ; but with the small-holder it is often his one and only field that the entire Hunt comes tearing over.

12

I did once put in a claim against the Staghounds for damage done to a hedge, for the making of which by stakes and woven hazels I had just paid two men £2. Again they were hunting the stag, and those who followed the hounds were such poor riders that they could not clear this low hedge, but burst through it, leaving an ugly gap through which my neighbour's sheep soon entered into my water-meadow. Of course no attempt was ever made to repair the gap, any more than any attempt was ever made to repair the broken-down eve-gate. Such courtesies are not traditional with hunting people.

I promptly sent in a claim which brought within my gate the Master of the Staghounds. He and another well-known hunting man drove up in a smart dogcart, and I was intensely amused at the manner in which the M.S.H., who comes of an old county family and *does* know the difference between seeds and stubble, tried to flatter me by referring to those fellows who rode through my hedge as being a lot of "damned stockbrokers." I held, however, to my claim, which was paid, and as the two gentlemen were about to drive away I remarked :

"Don't you think that you might have

informed these stockbrokers that we resent their riding across our fields and gardens just as much as they would resent it if I rode over their tennis-court and through their kitchen garden ?   It really comes to the same thing."

Out of the saddle no one could have been more courteous than this gentleman.   It is curious the difference that being booted and spurred makes to the ordinary English country gentleman.

Both these gentlemen laughed, when about to drive away, as I reminded them of Oscar Wilde's *bon mot* in describing fox-hunting as " the unspeakable after the uneatable." But the laughter rang a little hollow as it echoed down the farm road.

The arrogant insolence of the sporting " gentry " is really remarkable.   In a village where I once lived, a village in which curt-seying was practised with much agility, the squire, who drove some spirited horses, used to send out a runner before the carriage to warn the village women to keep their children inside their garden gates, because they might startle the horses !   The overlord was about to pass out in his carriage-and-pair.   Per-haps, though, this notification was not so coolly presumptuous as the warning on the board placed by a roadside hedge near Grey-well, Hants.

```
PLEASE
DRIVE CAUTIOUSLY.
HOUND PUPPIES
ARE AT WALK IN
GREYWELL VILLAGE.
```

Hound puppies, mark you : *not* village children. The board, surely, faithfully registers the mind of those who are filled with the lust of sport.

The Big Bag

Before passing on to the subject of game-preserving I should like to dispel a widespread illusion which the methods of fox-hunters have fostered that the traditions of feudal England are still law with respect to fox-hunting. People still seem to imagine that those who ride to hounds to hunt vermin such as the fox have the legal right to trespass over your ground. This is not so. It is done on the assumption only that you permit them to ride over your fields.

Photograph of the notice board with its solicitous care for the welfare of the Puppies. A school is near.

To face page 173.

Thus, in Paul *versus* Summerhayes, 1875, a case was fought out in the courts of law. The respondent warned off those engaged in fox-hunting and resisted their entrance on his field by force. The booted and spurred were charged with committing an assault, of which they were convicted. It is interesting to note, however, that the farm belonged to the respondent's father. Had he been a tenant-farmer we should probably never have had this case to cite. Upon appeal to the Court of Queen's Bench the conviction was affirmed, and Lord Coleridge, then Chief Justice, laid down that the sport of fox-hunting must be carried on in subordination to the ordinary rights of property.

In the course of his judgment he said: " Questions such as the present fortunately [I should have said, unfortunately] do not arise, because those who pursue the sport of fox-hunting do so in a reasonable spirit[!], and only go upon the lands of those whose consent is expressly, or may be assumed to be tacitly, given. There is no principle of law that justifies trespassing over the lands of others for the purposes of fox-hunting."

In the case of Baker *versus* Berkeley, 1827 it was shown that if a person who keeps hounds receives notice not to trespass on the lands of others, and after this his hounds run

out upon those lands followed by a number of
other persons, the owner of the hounds will be
answerable for all the damage such persons do,
even though he himself forbears to go upon
the lands in question, unless he has distinctly
warned them not to go on those lands.

It is quite permissible by law to shoot or
trap a fox, and in the neighbourhood of Street
in Somersetshire, where there are many small
owners and a great many poultry-keepers,
the Co-operative Poultry Depot will reward
with 5s. anyone who brings in a fox's head.
But spirited action like this is only evinced
in a neighbourhood like Street, where there is
a large boot factory, with many independent
cultivators of holdings—or where there is a
spirited woman.

At Street the poultry industry is considered
of far more importance to the inhabitants,
and to the nation as a whole, than fox-hunting ;
and in the neighbourhood of Evesham, where
there are nearly 10,000 acres taken up in small
holdings, a rabbit has a small chance of life if
it ever shows its nose on a cabbage plot.

The rise of the new race of small-holders is
every year diminishing the area dominated
by hordes of barbarians that hunt the stag
or fox, and let us hope that, when agriculture
is more seriously pursued by this nation, the
hordes will be confined to certain areas as

their hunting field, like the Apache Indian in the Western States of America.

Though there may be something to be said for fox-hunting—for the riders do at any rate risk breaking their necks, especially nowadays, with the almost universal use of the barbed wire—what is there to be said in favour of game-preserving on a princely scale, and of the modern battue?

There is nothing more dreaded in any countryside where agriculture is seriously practised than the descent upon the neighbourhood of a very wealthy man who desires to win social distinction by getting up some very big shoots. A whole parish can become easily demoralised in a very short time and agriculture sink into decay; for instead of seeking an honest day's work men will look out for the job of beating by day and of poaching by night. A company of non-producers will soon devour the crops of the producers. Soon, too, will the petty tyranny exercised by the head gamekeeper and the under-keepers over those who labour in the fields be felt by both Hodge and his master.

Hodge already feels that the gentleman in blue promenades the highways to watch *him*; already is resentfully conscious of the searching eye of the policeman cast upon him even when returning home with a bag over his shoulder, though it may contain but a few hedging tools. And now, with the advent of a great game-preserve, there is a gentleman in velveteens throwing furtive glances after him down the byways. The pleasant green road betwixt high hedges is no longer to him the primrose path starred with the wild flower, where he may rest awhile to eat his bread and cheese, for behind every hedge now is a pair of eyes watching him, especially if he has the audacity to take his own dog out for a walk in the cool twilight after the heat and burthen of the day. His children's favourite cat is sure to be shot by some gamekeeper before it is a month old. No wonder that he feels an outcast in his own land : no wonder he sighs when he thinks of the young fellows' stories of Canada and Australia that he hears in the tap-room of "The Spotted Cow." He, however, can never make the break for freedom : the chains of feudalism have gripped him too firmly.

If he has always been suspected of poaching by these spies of the rich men his *moral* in time will be undermined. He will drop his industrious habits and will join the ranks of the casual labourers. It is an easier way of living, to make 3s. by a few hours' beating and get a thumb-piece and a pint of beer thrown in, than to work for 2s. 6d. for a long day in following the plough, without the thumb-piece of bread and cheese and the pint of beer thrown in. Beside, in loafing about there is always the possibility of " tips " falling like manna from heaven.

With the swooping down in motor cars from Town of large parties of rich men, the glitter of wealth is omnipresent, and as it dazzles it dries up the sources of wealth at the fount.

Then so thick upon the ground becomes the game that the labourer may feel, as he sees farm crops being destroyed by game, that if he can evade the law nothing but good can result from a nocturnal visit to the woods. He might earn in one night more than he could earn by a whole week's hard labour to keep his family from starvation.

Even the farmer feels the restriction on his liberty by game-preserving.

" It destroys his self-respect," wrote Mr. John Bright, " and the independence of his character. He takes a farm and contracts to pay a rent; he stocks it with cattle and sheep ; he ploughs, and sows, and reaps : *his landlord also stocks the same farm with hares, rabbits, and pheasants*, and enjoys his battue or sends to market the game which his tenant's produce has fed. The tenant has his servants to superintend or conduct the operations of his farm, and to feed and protect his cattle and his flocks : *the landlord has his keepers to secure his game* ; and these keepers are a spy upon the tenant himself, and traverse his fields by day and night, as though superior to his servants and himself. There are thus constituted to the same lands, and on the same property, two interests which must ever be diametrically opposed to each other—that of the cultivator and that of the game-preserver ; and out of this discord is sure to be engendered, and in thousands of cases failure and ruin to the weaker party.

" In all this there is a fruitful source of degradation to the farmer. Men of capital and independent feeling will shun an occupation which involves so much of humiliation, or they will protest against a system so prejudicial to the country, and so destructive of the character of those who are subjected to it."

I would that farmers took up a definite stand against the strong, instead of uniting as they invariably do against the weak. Unfortunately, if they feel the pressure from above, instead of manfully resisting it, they sullenly strike at those that are below. The losses from game-preserving to farmers as a class and to the nation as a whole are very great. *The Standard Encyclopædia of Modern Agriculture,* edited by Professor Wright, is a work in which the bias of articles concerning the economics of land-holding certainly leans towards the landed aristocracy, and yet in the article under the heading of "Game Preservation" we found the following record of tenant-farmers who gave evidence before Mr. Bright's committee.

Another village being deserted. Three of the four cottages are empty, decaying ; the fourth is occupied by a gamekeeper. Pheasants are of more interest to the landowner than peasants.

To face page 187.

M. B., farming in Hertfordshire, detailed the particulars of damage on his farm, and gave in an award drawn up by two arbitrators in which the injury committed by the game during one season on land not exceeding 35 acres was upwards of £118. He stated also that the damage he sustained on the whole of his farm was equal to an increased rent of £200 a year.

Mr. C., farming more than 3,000 acres, arable and sheep walk, in the county of Norfolk, stated that he was the loser of nearly £1,000 by the damage done by game. The greatest damage was in the wheat crop, but grass and sainfoin were also much injured. At the commencement of his lease about 500 hares were killed yearly ; but last year they killed at —— 2,500 hares, and he considered that 2,000 of them were maintained by himself, his farm being nearer to the covert than the rest of the parish.

On a farm in Hertfordshire a single hen pheasant during the months of March and April destroyed as much of a piece of beans as amounted altogether to a quarter acre before she could be trapped. In this instance the pheasant found shelter in an adjoining wood. The bird pulled up the plants when they were about two inches high, that she might get at the bean at the root.

This evidence, of course, was given some years ago, but as the passion on the part of the *nouveaux riches* to obtain big bags in order to tempt royalty to shoot over their estates has been on the increase, if Parliamentary evidence were taken to-day it would assuredly show still more startling facts against game-preserving.

188 TYRANNY OF THE COUNTRYSIDE

In his book, *Land Problems*, published only last year, Mr. Christopher Turnor, who is a large Lincolnshire landowner and a Conservative, makes this statement :

The amount of money spent on shooting, in spite of the decrease of revenue, is far greater than it used to be ; the preserving and raising of game has been reduced to a science, and the lust of big bags has taken possession of men who often can ill afford the sport, and who endeavour to compete with the standard set by richer men who take shootings in the neighbourhood . . .

No amount of monetary compensation can make up for the discouragement to the farmer and the harm done to the routine of a farm by having a considerable number of acres of barley destroyed by game. I have been over farms in which not only a large proportion of the root crop, but every single swede and mangold has been damaged by hares. . . . I have heard landowners, men who ought to know better, say of such and such a farm that it was only fit to rear game. There are very few farms of which this could be in any wise true.

I myself constantly traverse an estate by a public footpath. It is an estate of some 300 acres, which, with the old timbered house, has been in the market for a number of years. It once belonged to a country squire, but a divorce suit occurring and a death happening, the estate was sold to a syndicate of land speculators who have held it up, so to speak, for ten years, waiting for a rise in land values.

The timbered house and the shooting is the attraction, but, the price set upon the place being exorbitant, it has not been sold.   Once a year a mowing machine passes over the grass fields of this park-land, and in winter its woods resound with the shots of the guns.   Year by year this good agricultural land is depreciating in value as agricultural land, and year by year its price as site value is rising.   But the nation grows no richer.   On the contrary, as far as the workers are concerned it grows poorer, for so abundant have been the rabbits and so devastating have been their inroads upon the meadow grass that this year only three loads of hay have been gathered in a nine-acre meadow.   The estate is solely used, with the timbered house standing empty, as a pleasure resort for sporting cockneys.   Surely it would be better to see in place of a man in velveteens, accoutred like the hero of a comic opera, a gang of strenuous workers swinging the scythe amid the lush grass, and, instead of the keeper's one assistant, a team of lusty pitchers gathering from billowing winrows a largesse of fragrant hay, and filling a fully manned wagon before an acre is swept clean.

The pathetic part about Mr. Turnor's book is that he makes an appeal as a landowner to other landowners to relinquish in the national interest some of their shooting.   That is the one thing for which the landowners of England, in their love for sport, will shoulder their guns to the last ditch to defend.

" It is to be regretted," says Mr. Turnor, "that the Act (Land Holdings Act of 1907) does little to protect a small farmer from excessive damage by game. It provides, in the case of a farmer with land adjacent to coverts, that reasonable compensation shall be paid for damage done by pheasants ; but in the event of rabbits coming out of the said coverts in their thousands and devastating the surrounding farms, the farmer can put in no claim— the Ground Game Act is supposed to afford him sufficient protection. It does not, however, do so. Take the case of a small farmer, whose whole time should be given to the cultivation of the soil : how can he find opportunity to snare rabbits or to shoot them ? On the first shot the rabbits all retire to the wood, where he cannot follow them. A large farmer can employ a rabbit-catcher ; this a small farmer cannot do."

I know this very well from my own experience as a small farmer. Not only can one ill afford to engage someone to shoot, snare, or ferret out rabbits, but it rarely pays the individual to take advantage of the wonderful privileges conceded by the Ground Game Act. Many a time I have gone down, as Mr. Turnor suggests, at dusk when rabbits begin to come out of their burrows to feed on my grass, which I can ill afford to see devoured on a pasture of only eight acres.

With a single-barrel gun I can only reduce their number by one, and with a double-barrelled gun there is only a sporting chance of reducing the number by two after having waited, gun in hand, for a whole hour. This sounds as though rabbits could not be very plentiful, but it must be remembered that they are scared at your first appearance in the field, and it is some time even after you have taken up an advantageous position in the lee of the wind before they will venture out again from their burrows.

Though I live in a district where only a moderate amount (according to modern landowners' ideas) of game-preserving exists, I lost seventy young apple trees, the bark of which was gnawed by hares and rabbits one winter's night. I had already gone to the expense of ordering the wire-netting to protect the trees from the depredations of the hares and rabbits, but a hard winter's frost overtook us, and brought hungry hares to the plantation before the netting had been fixed completely round.

It is very hard, surely, that a cultivator should, in any case, have to go to all the expense and labour to protect his crops against the game from the rich man's preserves, and even when wire-netting is erected rabbits and hares will often either burrow under or leap over it. Many a time have I lost my winter greens—not simply a few plants, but the entire crop; and I have now given up as hopeless the growing of winter wheat or oats.

Apologists for the present conditions of life of the agricultural labourer often point, and rightly enough, to the help that allotments are to labourers in the way of supplying their families with food. Where, however, game is strictly preserved this benefit is often reduced to a vanishing-point. Take the case of Ridgmount, a village in Bedfordshire, of which Mr. P. H. Mann has written so intimately in his *Life in an Agricultural Village in England*, published in the Sociological Papers :

In view of the fact that a great deal has been made of the profits to be made by holdings and allotments, it is interesting to have obtained the views of some of those who hold them in the village. This particular village is, however, not quite a typical case, for most of the allotments lie too close to the Duke of Bedford's park, where game is strictly preserved ; and the result is that havoc is usually wrought among the crops sown. Corn of any sort is in fact rarely grown here, and the crops are limited to potatoes and a few other vegetables.

Mr. Mann also mentions that neither the keeping of pigs nor of poultry is encouraged by the Duke of Bedford ; possibly there is some subtle connection between the nasal organs of big shooting parties and cottagers' piggeries. In this case, however, the prohibition against pig-keeping is not so great a loss to the cottager as it might be in some other villages, for to keep pigs profitably it is necessary to grow barley for the straw as well as for the grain, and to grow barley on the allotments at Ridgmount is a disastrous proceeding, as it would be destroyed by game.

Although the Ground Game Act graciously permits in England the farmer to shoot hares on his own land, there are many small farmers who are expected by those who have hired or hold the shooting to leave the hares untouched. I have already mentioned the instance of a landlord of the South Downs who expects his tenants not even to touch the rabbits which overrun the farm.

No farmer who takes the business of agriculture seriously regards rabbit-burrows on his farm as any economic advantage to him, and in places where game-preserving has been practised with great severity I have known the gamekeeper deliberately raise the bottom of the farmer's wire-netting with his boot in order that he may rear more heads of game at the farmer's expense.

Where, too, pressure is put upon the gamekeepers by their employers, the temptation

13

for other gamekeepers to turn poacher is very considerable, and I have known of game-preservers who have actually bought eggs that have been laid in their own woods.

In spite, too, of modifications of the Game Laws, there is still a strong fear in the minds of agricultural labourers against touching anything that belongs to the sacred bird. I remember a labourer who had been mowing some grass for me, close to a spinny where I kept some hens, finding some pheasants' eggs in a hen's nest. Although these were laid on my ground, he came and told me of their presence in an awestruck voice, as though he were a smuggler telling me of the hiding-place of some keg of brandy.

Game Laws, formulated of course by a landlord class, oppressive as they still are in England, are more tyrannical in Liberal Scotland and Nationalist Ireland. In Scotland, for instance, there is still in force an old Act which dates back to 1621, whereby it is enacted that no one may kill game who is not the owner of a ploughgate of land (about 100 acres) situate in Scotland. There, too, the right of shooting depends not, as in England, on the occupancy of land, but on the ownership. Furthermore, in Scotland, a farmer could be convicted of being unlawfully on his own farm at night for the purpose of killing game. That this amazing piece of feudal legislation is still in force, I learn from the article on " Game Law" in the *Standard Encyclopædia of Modern Agriculture*. You need not even be seen on your land to be convicted, for it has been held that an offence under the Act may be committed by remaining on the road and sending a dog on to the land in pursuit of game or by shooting on to the land from the road without actual entry on to it, and any servant of the farmer or other person who remains in the road to give the alarm is equally guilty of entering some-one's land for the purpose of killing game. Indeed, the series of Game and Trespass Acts applicable to Scotland are almost incon-ceivable in this twentieth century.

In Ireland, too, one can hardly realise that no one is allowed to kill hares, pheasants, partridges, grouse, or quails, unless he owns freehold land to the yearly value of £40, or personal estate of the value of £1,000.

In the face of these facts it will be a very long time before either Liberal or Conserva-tive politicians will dispel the labourer's im-pression that there is one law for the rich and another for the poor.

CHAPTER VII

THE PERSONAL IN POLITICS

THERE is a piquancy in politics in Arcadia, the savour of which is quite unknown in large and crowded cities. If a pertinent quip, a riposte, a challenging note that has often been the undoing of pompous speakers, is uttered from the body of the hall in an urban political meeting, it is invariably reported as "a Voice." In the village school-room it is quite different. Here it is "Why, that's old Bill Smith," or "Shut your clapper, Tom," and the speaker on the platform, unless he be an outside carpet-bagger, will invariably address the interrupter by name.

I have experienced a good deal of the personal element in local rural politics, and to assure my readers that I write with no personal animus I shall dwell on the humorous side of parochial politics in which I have been a partaker.

Personally, I have suffered no martyrdom, nor have I ever been denied hospitality at the houses of either the rich or the poor, save possibly at the homes of a few ponderously dull and rich people. Somehow I have managed to get on sociably with both landowners and farmers—the two classes with whom I have had most to enter into conflict; and in more than one parish I have had the assistance of the enlightened landowners to fight the farmer-councillor-employer class over its domination of the labouring poor.

It is easier for me to appreciate the humorous side of things than for other rural workers, as my livelihood is not dependent on the goodwill of those round about me. The pen rather than the shepherd's crook has been my staff of life. That has made all the difference in the world. Only once did things look grave for me, and that was when I had to leave one house and seek another roof in the same parish. Then it was that I had against my will to buy the cottage in which I afterwards lived.

I shall never forget my first entrance into public life as a Parish Councillor. It was in a village where all the farmers were of one family. They not only rented all the farms, but possessed the butcher's shop, ran the laundry, owned the local waterworks, and most of the insanitary cottages. They sat on the Parish Council, the Rural District Council, and the County Council. A network of oppression was drawn completely over the lives of the poor of this parish.

Without hesitation I hoisted my Jolly Roger in the form of a printed sheet, issued monthly, in which I exposed the local abuses. As it may be imagined, I was carrying a good deal of sail, but I determined to effect a passage through the heavily armoured and hostile fleet. I had one supreme advantage, and that was my black-and-white sheet. I managed to run the blockade successfully, but when I got into port I found I had only one friend, and he was a doctor and an Irishman. He happened to be the reigning chairman of the Council. The six farmers and the other local doctor, who happened to be their medical attendant, determined to put their own nominee in the chair. One of them proposed the name of the new chairman. He was the father and uncle of several of the farmers present, and also vice-chairman of the Rural District Council. Incidentally, he was chairman of the waterworks and owner of several insanitary cottages to which the water was not laid on. The proposition was seconded and carried. My doctor friend, naturally enough, feeling hurt, left the chair and the room, never to enter it again.

I was thus left alone with six charming companions who agreed amongst themselves that one of them should be sent on an embassy to the patriarch who had been appointed chairman. He soon returned to make the oracular statement that "father's taken off his boots." My companions, who looked like a lot of sulky tribal chieftains who thought they had been honouring highly their sultan, instructed the son to explain to his father the extent of the honour they had done him. So we sat in silence for about ten minutes. I think a smile must have been hovering round my lips as I gazed at their mean countenances, and when the benevolent patriarch, with rubicund face and white whiskers, eventually entered the room, he said in the most innocent way, "Did you want me, gentlemen?" I think he would have made his mark on the stage.

He had made a boast that he had never read the Parish Councils Act, and what is more, never intended to. However, that was no drawback to my fellow-councillors, and when I immediately proposed that the Rural District Council should put into force at once the Housing of the Working Classes Act, 1890, every one of my fellow-councillors (being for the most part interested in cottage property) unanimously agreed that there was no need for any new cottages. Before the next monthly meeting took place I hoisted

again my Jolly Roger, and then, as the cheer-
ful cockney would say, "the band began to
play."

I had visited the old patriarch's insanitary
cottages at night, for the tenants did not wish
me to be seen entering them by day. I saw
by the light of a lantern the slimy, green pool
which formed their only water-supply. The
funny part was that the only way to get to
this pond unseen was through an orchard, also
owned by the chairman of the Council. With
me went a friend, an ardent reformer, who was
a clerk at the local mill. The next evening
the chairman's son, who sat on the Council,
met me in the village and asked me if I had
seen anyone entering his father's orchard, for,
said he, he thought he had seen me riding a
bicycle past it.

"Oh yes," I answered cheerfully, "I was
by there last night."

"There were two of you," he said eagerly,
"weren't there?"

I saw at once what he wanted. He wanted
me to mention the name of the friend who
was with me, and thus attempt to bring about
his dismissal from his employment.

"I didn't see any other bicycle," I said
(my friend was walking). "But why do you
want to know? Have you missed any apples,"
I said laughingly.

" Ye-es." He moved awkwardly.

" How many ? " I asked.

" About a bushel," came the lame answer.

" Why, you must be as good a judge of apples as you are of beef, to miss a bushel from so large an orchard," I answered, laughing at him.

Now not only did I describe in my little paper the conditions of the local cottages, but I also held a public meeting in the village street.

Then things began to get thoroughly tuned up. Soon after this a friend overheard a group of councillors consulting with one another as to whether I ought to have a " good thrashing with a horse-whip or be chucked into a horse-pond." Then someone suggested taking my " rag," as my little paper was politely called, to a firm of solicitors in the nearest little town, to see if a slander action could not be instituted against me. Instead, however, of a libel action being brought against me, on the eve of another election I proposed again that the Housing of the Working Classes Act should be put into force ; and not only was this seconded, but it was carried under the lowering eye of our chairman !

The Jolly Roger had triumphed, but—the resolution had to go before the Rural District Council, and our chairman was the vice-chairman of that body. It was he who after all, had the last smile—had that wily old fox.

It is when the Parliamentary elections take place that we get a higher pulse in the political arena and more pungent personal encounters.

At a recent general election a lady who owns several thousand acres, whom I shall call Miss Bray, took a very active part. She spoke, I remember, at a meeting of local landowners who had come together to consider the wretched land taxes—taxes which would affect them but little, as most of them were owners of agricultural land.

Nevertheless, they were filled with a social unrest. They hoisted the flag of revolution and they asked the poor labourers, herded at one end of the schoolroom like sheep in a cattle-pen, to join them. They spoke to them like brothers. " It is you men," they said, " who will suffer most. That is why we have come together to consider these iniquitous taxes. We owners of property can always dodge them. But you, you will lose your work by the reduction of establishments," etc., etc. Miss Bray then donned the cap of liberty, and after politely describing Mr. Lloyd George as a low-bred man of a race noted for lying, went on to explain how, if *she* were Chancellor of the Exchequer, *she* would raise the revenue in order to build our *Dreadnoughts*. First and foremost, she would tax all those tramp-perambulators filled with dirty babies which infest our country lanes and highways !

Advanced movements, great political names, come very little under the cognisance of labourers and their wives who never see a daily paper and rarely see a weekly one. When they do read these it is more often than not the police news, the divorce court scandals, and the racing, in *Lloyd's News* and *The People*, that hold their attention. I find Radical cottagers often read *The People* without being in the least aware that it is a Tory journal, and Tory labourers reading *Lloyd's News* without knowing that they are reading a Liberal journal, which is perhaps not to be wondered at. It is true that a man who reads his *Reynolds* may be a politician, but to the ordinary cottager the provisions of the Insurance Act, the Clauses in the Town Planning Act, discussions on the amendments of the Small Holdings Act, might be written in some dead language as far as these are understandable by the country people unversed in letters. Just as they are rarely glib of tongue, so are they rarely quick readers of the printed sheet. It is not that they lack intelligence. It is simply because

they are untrained, by living lives of manual
toil, spent in isolation amid wide spaces
from an early age, that they are inexpert
in following the printed word or in express-
ing themselves in the language of the classes
that have book-learning. I regard it as one
of the greatest triumphs of my life that my
paper was welcomed at every cottage door,
though its entrance there meant the forfeit-
ing of one halfpenny out of small earnings.
It was, I think, the only "advanced"
literature that these cottagers had ever
read outside the gospels and the epistle of
St. James.

Townsmen would be appalled at the indifference of most country labourers to the
existence of prominent political personages.
On one winter's day two men, who were both
Conservatives by tradition, were digging for
me. Somehow Keir Hardie's name cropped
up. " Why, I thought he was dead and done
for," said one of them, shoving his spade into
the half-frozen earth. I explained to them
that Keir Hardie was very much alive just
then, for he was undergoing what I believe is
called " a rag " in Cambridge, and if I remember rightly he had to leave that town
without his world-famed deer-stalker.

Quite recently I mentioned Miss Christabel
Pankhurst's disappearance to a cottage woman.

" Who may she be ? " she asked me.
They may know who Lloyd George is, but
Bonar Law they imagine to be some Act of
Parliament.

Far removed from the literary track of
ideas, to most country labourers in southern
England there are only two parties—the two
historic parties.   To the countryman, the
farmer in particular, a Socialist for instance
is a kind of resident of Sidney Street who has
had to be smoked out by gunpowder.

In my own parish a Socialist, who is a boot-
maker, recently took up his residence.   Like
most Socialists he began to promulgate his
views with a zealous activity.   One of the
victims of his oratory was a farmer and a
member of the Parish Council—a Parish
Council which consists of one Liberal,
who is the village grocer, and eight Conservative farmers and publicans.   They are
altogether a very united and happy family,
presided over by the schoolmaster, who is an
interesting specimen of quite a prehistoric
Tory.   The Liberal grocer is a man who
shakes his head at Mr. Lloyd George and does
not like the savour of Shop Acts or Insurance
Acts, all of which restrict " the liberty of
the individual," he complains, and on the ex-
piration of their term of office as Parochial
Councillors it was only natural that the Liberal

grocer should offer to get the nomination papers filled for one of the Conservative councillors. This gentleman happened to be the farmer who had been the unhappy recipient of the full-blooded oratory of the Socialist newcomer. The grocer instructed his assistant on his rounds with the cart to get the farmer's nomination papers filled in by a proposer and a seconder, and the assistant, thinking that one name was as good as another, obtained as a proposer the name of a farmer and as a seconder the name of the Socialist, who happened to be the second customer on his rounds. The Socialist, I am sure, must have signed the document with the spirit of mischief hovering round as the evil genius.

" I got your paper filled up, Mr. Giles," said the youthful assistant proudly. " That's right," said the farmer, glad to be saved the trouble of taking it round himself. But when his eye lighted upon the name of his seconder he fell into a demoniacal rage, called his wife to witness the awful act of sacrilege, and tearing the paper into many strips, yelled out, " Why, that name would lose me a hundred votes! That man's an atheist! That man's an annichrist! That man's a *vegetarian*! "

In the realm of local politics I once had a delightful experience. I ran for a Council larger than a Parish Council. To my surprise

I polled 181 votes, and I found that quite 75 per cent. of these votes were due not to my programme, which would certainly have raised the rates and was therefore highly unpopular, but to the fact that my bowling average for the local cricket club showed the best record !

To illustrate how long it takes labourers, who live even within forty miles of London, to realise that there is any other party in the State but the Liberal and Tory parties, I will relate an amusing incident that happened to myself.

One of those Tariff Reform vans (which I believe can now be bought up cheaply by gipsies) entered our village, and stood on the grassy plot in front of the rectory gates. Almost the entire village, rich and poor, was present. The Tariff Reform lecturer had spoken very well, and after him followed one of the local " gentry "—a retired brewer. His sole contribution to economics and to world-wide statecraft consisted of these words:

" Men, you all know *me* " ("Hear, hear ! " " He's a jolly good fellow ! ")

" Well, all I ask of you is to be men—be men." And he sat down amid vociferous cheering.

His speech certainly had the virtue of brevity ; but I felt that the crowd still looked mentally hungry-eyed, and I, a new-comer in the village, rashly ventured to give them something more substantial to think about. I addressed the chairman, whom I happened to know. " Colonel ——, may I say a few words ? "

" Certainly," he answered warmly, being under the delusion that I was a Tariff Reformer.

I mounted the van and told the hungry-eyed crowd that we three—the brewer, the Colonel, and myself—were revolutionaries. We all three wanted a change.

At this I was aware that the brewer spluttered out something to the chairman, and as I proceeded to talk, my subconscious-ness informed me that the brewer was wildly expostulating with the chairman for allowing me to go on, and the gallant Colonel would repeatedly answer, " I cannot help it. I *must* let him finish *now*."

On the outskirts of the little crowd one or two began to see the agitation of their generous friend, the brewer. The publican began to be disturbed, and the cry was raised, " Pull 'im down ! Chuck 'im out ! "

" Now then, fair dews," came the retort from one or two of the more stalwart politi-cians.

I said what I wanted to say. I told them

that we were all at war with one another :
the landlord was squeezing as much rent as
he could out of the farmer, the farmer as
much work as he could out of the labourer,
the labourer giving as little as he need
for low wages, and that neither political
party presented a programme to end this
internecine strife. We should have to form
a new party to do that—a Labour Party.

My heterodox speech had to be dispelled
from the minds of the hearers by the calling
for lusty cheers for the brewer, the King, and
the Empire.

The next morning a friend of mine asked
a Liberal labourer what he thought of the
speeches.

"Darned lot o' vules," laconically responded the labourer.

"But you heard Green's speech?" said
my friend with a little enthusiasm, expecting
that in me at any rate the labourer would
see a comrade.

"Why, he be the biggest vule of the lot,"
came the crushing comment. "*He wants a
new party !*"

14

CHAPTER VIII

THE LADY AND THE VOTER

IT is a curious reflection that it is the gentler sex which has figured the more prominently in criminal cases under the Corrupt Practices Act. This is not because women, even women with property, are more tyrannical than men in the misuse of their economic position, but because they have been ignorant of the provisions of the Corrupt Practices Act. They have generally committed themselves for trial through writing a letter, a mistake which male landlords are careful enough to avoid, and which is one reason why intimidation is so difficult a thing to run to earth.

The Corrupt Practices Act, framed to prevent undue influence, might just as well have never become law, for no jury has yet been found to harden its heart, after centuries of political corruption, to condemn anyone to one year's imprisonment with or without hard labour.

Although an evicted tenant, or one that is boycotted, may have to suffer semi-starvation for many months because he has dared to think for himself and express any opinions at all, yet few of us would care to punish, were we on a jury, in so severe a manner, even those who struck so mean a blow. If you turn to provincial papers in the last year or two you will find reports of cases where letters have been read in court such as the following, which I take from the *Western Morning News*, October 28, 1910; but you will not find a single instance of a jury finding the accused guilty.

A lady who was a landowner, living at a Devonshire parsonage, writes to a thatcher who occupied one of her cottages at a rent of £4 a year thus :

DAVEY,—I was surprised to see my door placarded with Liberal papers. I hope you won't allow this to happen again, and I also hope you will not support Lambert against me as a landowner, as I would not have any tenant who went against me.

Davey, it is needless to add, had to go, and take another cottage. It was some time before he could find one. The lady, apparently to her great amazement, found herself served with a writ, and had to appear at the Exeter Assizes to defend her action, and after a little severe lecturing by the judge, who, I believe, was a strong Conservative, was allowed to go back to her country parsonage.

Of course Davey never instituted the action; a poor thatcher who pays a rent of £4 a year is not in a position to bring a legal action against a landowner to whom he is indebted for the roof over his head and a good deal of his daily bread. That, surely, is all the more reason why landowners should live up to the aristocratic motto, " Noblesse oblige," and never interfere with the political opinions of their tenants, as is the commendable practice of Mr. A. J. Balfour.

Without a political organisation behind Davey the case would never have been heard of. We wonder how many cases of intimidation are suffered in silence by the poor?

There was another interesting little case which never got beyond the Grand Jury, which was reported in the *Standard* for July 4, 1910:

" You must not expect to walk any more pups for me," wrote a lady frankly to a villager, " as I consider it my clear duty to help those who put their country, Church, and children's education before their party."

No doubt the pups are now attended by someone who will with due subservience reflect the political complexion of the mistress of the puppies, so that she may feel she is helping through them her country and her Church, to say nothing of the children's education.

We will now pass on to the case of a railwayman of Speen, in Berkshire, who rented a cottage from two ladies. This man had the audacity to exhibit Liberal bills in his window, and on his insisting upon exercisng his rights as a free-born Briton he was given notice to quit. Not being a farm-labourer and dependent upon his landlord-employer for his living, he stiffened his back and refused to go. Two actions were immediately started against him by his two landladies, one in the County Court and the other in the Petty Sessions. The bench of magistrates, in view of the fact that proceedings had been commenced elsewhere, refused to make any order. At the County Court, Judge Harrington, while granting the necessary order for eviction, said : " People are entitled to their political opinions, provided they do not interfere with anybody else. And if these ladies did so act—and I certainly cannot help having some suspicions that they did— it was a very discreditable thing." Yet to defend his rights as a citizen this man, Mr. G. Gardner, incurred heavy legal expenses. These, I am happy to say, were returned to him by the Gladstone League, but he lost his home, and had to walk three and a half miles daily to his work.

Then there is the story of the shepherd of Tingewick, part of which only has been made public. The farm was managed by the son-in-law of the landlady. He told the shepherd one Saturday, when paying him his wages, that he would have to leave, as his mother-in-law objected to his politics. A friend of mine called upon the son-in-law, who stated that he was sorry to lose the shepherd, who was a very good one, but that his mother-in-law had strong political convictions, though he himself did not think politics were worth bothering about. He admitted that it was a hard case, but there was nothing to be done.

Both in this case and in another which occurred recently in a Hertfordshire village, it was the man who managed the estate rather than the lady who owned it who showed to the better advantage. The latter case, in which an estate woodman was discharged by the lady owner because of his political opinions, was never pressed beyond a certain point in a court of law as a criminal charge, because the bailiff was prepared to tell the truth, which would have militated against his mistress. She denied using undue influence ; and those who were responsible for the prosecution decided not to demand so great a price in personal sacrifice on the part of the bailiff, who would assuredly have lost his post.

The knowledge of the misuse of their position made by women who own the soil does not in the least militate against my strong conviction that all women should be admitted to the same rights of citizenship as men. On the other hand, these glaring, ugly facts I have adduced intensify my convictions. With a larger political education, half-educated ladies will perhaps gain wider knowledge, and with it greater sympathy for the lives of the workers. There is no doubt that a limited Women's Suffrage Bill will become law in the very near future, but what I want to see made law is that Hodge's wife should have a vote, too. Indeed, it would be more just as things stand now that the lady landowner who now controls, without the vote, the lives of so many people, should remain voteless, and the labourer's wife should be given the small crumb of satisfaction of being able to vote for measures which shall place a scrape of butter on the dry bread she has hitherto given to her children.

The treatment by wealthy ladies in the country of those who toil is extraordinary to anyone who knows the point of view of those classes. I think Mr. Jerome K. Jerome was quite right in saying that if the poor hated the rich half as much as the rich hate the poor, then God help the rich ! I remember he said this just at the time when I was trying to get a list started in my own village containing signatures in favour of a Suffrage Bill for Women. It was quite pathetic to find that the poorer the male voter the more anxious he was that the Bill should give the lady of property the vote, whilst his own wife should remain voteless. Possibly this is only peculiar, and let us hope it is, to the rural districts of southern England, which even to-day, in the twentieth century, have not yet emerged from the desolating twilight of the feudal age.

The church at Combe, Hants, where the vicar was locked out for three Sundays because he told his churchwardens they spent more on market days on themselves in victuals and drink than they paid their carters for the week's work.

To face page 217.

CHAPTER IX

THE PARSON AND THE LABOURER

Parson do preach and tell we to pray,
And to think of our work, and not ask more pay ;
And to follow ploughshare, and never think
Of crazy cottage and ditch-stuff's stink—
That Doctor do say breeds ager and chills,
Or, worse than that, the fever that kills—
And a' bids me pay my way like a man,
Whether I can't or whether I can ;
And as I ha'n't beef, to be thankful for bread,
And bless the Lord it ain't turmuts instead ;
And never envy the farmer's pig,
For all a' lies warm, and is fed so big,
While the missus and little uns grow that thin,
You may count their bones underneath the skin ;
I'm to call all I gets " the chastening rod,"
And look up to my betters and then thank God.

Punch.

MR. W. H. HUDSON, in his book *Afoot in England,* and I, in my book, *The Awakening of England* have told the story of how a Hampshire parson was locked out of his church for three Sundays because he dared to tell his churchwardens, even in the late Victorian era, that they spent more on their persons on market days than they paid their ploughman for a whole week's work. Mr.

Hudson had the story from the parson himself, whilst I had it from one of his parishioners. And though there is the exceptional spiritual shepherd, like this one of Combe, and the rector of Tockenham, in Wiltshire, we are perpetually confronted by the fact that the parson is hand in glove with the farmer and the landlord in keeping the poor in that station of life to which I, for one, am sure that it did not please God to call them.

Though in some parishes the parson is a man to be pitied for his struggling poverty, or loved for his burning zeal to succour the weak, there are unfortunately other clergymen who exercise tyrannical sway over village life, not only as vicar, but also as landlord, and as guardian of the poor. And the worst of it is, whenever there happens to be a good parson in a country parish, you will find that he will foolishly appoint as his churchwarden either the principal landowner or the large farmer of the parish, who is invariably not a friend of the poor. This is so often the case that labourers regard the triple alliance of squire, parson, and farmer as an inevitable if not a holy one. I suppose a labourer as a churchwarden is unknown in England.

As landlord of the glebe the parson, unfortunately, betrays the fact that he too is, after all, of the House of Rimmon. If you visit Sturminster (Dorset) you will find the allotments there are let at the rate of £8 an acre, and one small-holder has just received notice to quit because he refused to pay £10 a year for one and a half acres of grass land which was part of the glebe.

In another parish a new vicar gave his tenants notice to quit the allotments on his glebe, with the option of staying on at a rent more than that charged by his predecessor. When remonstrated with he told the labourers that he could easily let his land to the farmers. The men paid the increased rate, for, as one of them remarked to me, " they were so used to the thumb-screw that they had no energy left to resist it."

In the vale of the Avon I found a vicar asking such an exorbitant sum for his glebe-land, about to be purchased by the County Council for small holdings, that it was necessary to invoke the intervention of a Government arbitrator to award the price.

It is, however, as Guardian of the Poor, as dispenser of public as well as Church charities, that he can exercise the greatest power.

I once heard a very good parson say to another, " You ought to become a Guardian. The people have no respect for our sacerdotal office, but they have a great respect for us in the parish as Guardian."

The domination of the large farmer and the parson over the lives of the villagers is complete when, in addition to being landlords and employers, they are also school-managers, Parish Councillors, and Guardians of the Poor —or shall we say of the rates ?

I know a clergyman, for instance, who, having obtained a living by marriage, became elected as a Guardian of the Poor. On Sunday he would hold what services he deemed necessary. If he did not feel inclined to hold an evening service he would tell his parishioners so in the morning, stating simply that no evening service would be held for reasons which " he need not explain."

A few of the more ardent church-goers once asked him to give a children's service in the afternoon. The next Sunday morning in church he told his flock that they should bring their children to church with them in the morning " like this good woman here," pointing to a woman with her children in one of the front pews. On another Sunday he requested church-goers not to bring their dogs with them as far as the churchyard, as they fought with his dogs at the vicarage !

So much for him as a spiritual pastor. I will now recall a few of his deeds as a temporal master.

At the meetings of the Board of Guardians,

whenever there was a question of outdoor
relief, the amount decided upon as necessary
to keep body and soul together was invariably
fixed as if it were a sale of cattle at an auction
mart.

" How much shall we say, gentlemen ? "
the chairman would exclaim.   " Two-and-six,
three shillings, three-and-six, four shillings ?
Four shillings, did you say, Mr. Smith ? "

" I say," would interrupt our spiritual
pastor, " two-and-six is quite enough for this
person."

Then a smile would go round the Board.

" Yes, yes, quite so," the chairman would
say, " that is your *usual* opinion, Mr. ——.
Four shillings, gentlemen."

As an electioneering agent he displayed all
the old-world qualities.   He once called upon
a workman at his cottage to punish him for
what he called " his insolence."   On the man
opening his cottage door, the vicar promptly
knocked him down.   The workman's employer
happened to have no respect for his vicar, and
supported the workman in his charging the
vicar with assault.   The damages were settled
out of court.   On another occasion, when the
village butcher's pony entered one night the
hay-field of the vicar, he sent in a claim for
£20.

" What seemed to annoy him," said the

butcher to me, "was that I suggested that £2 might be deducted for damages off the big bill that he owed me."

Eventually, when the people of this parish, feeling ashamed of being represented on the Board of Guardians by a man of this type, urged upon the grocer, who was rather more independent than most village grocers, to stand in opposition to the vicar, he who felt himself the upholder of class tradition and the maintainer of the integrity of the British Empire issued an indignant protest against the effrontery of a " mere village tradesman " in opposing him.

Now I do not regard this man as typical of the Church of England clergy—not at all ; but what I wish to point out is that, if he is a bad man, he can be so thoroughly bad.

That there are clergymen who in championing the claims of the poor are frequently ostracised by the rich and scowled at by the farming class I am well aware. One such vicar, on a living of £150 a year, ran with me as a candidate for the Board of Guardians. The campaign of calumny which fastened on both of us left *me* unmoved; but, unfortunately, the richer parishioners made the life of my parson friend so unbearable that eventually he obtained an exchange of his living.

CHAPTER X

THE LABOURER AND HIS HIRE

" Labourer pour autrui, c'est un p'tit labourage ;
Faut labourer pour soi, c'est ça qui donn' courage."

THOSE who have always looked upon rural England as Arcadia—a place for the spending of quiet holidays, or a retreat for tired city brains, where the pulse of life beats with slow and pleasant precision, will, I am afraid, find the foregoing pages not pleasant to read.

"It is a little startling," wrote Mr. Punch, in reviewing my book, *The Awakening of England,* "to the indolent lover of solitude to find some exquisite and deserted landscape moving Mr. Green to fury."

That, I think, represents the feeling of the townsman towards the country. It is to him a retreat, and its quaint inhabitants were evidently placed there by Providence to gently minister to his sense of the ludicrous. To some "the country" is the place where one can take a morning gallop, shoulder a gun, handle a fishing-rod, or flourish a driving-iron. To others, as to Mr. Bernard Shaw, for instance, it is the district of fields and trees that lies at the end of flagged pavements where townsmen may take pleasant walks. To most, it is the landscape alone that fills the mental horizon ; a landscape in which the labourer appears as an adventitious figure.

By those few townsmen to whom the labourer appears like a spectre to haunt the uneasy conscience the terms of his hire are now being discussed.

In a recent correspondence which took place in the pages of the *Westminster Gazette*, some writers attempted to point out how much better off the country labourer was than the town labourer. One or two of them based their arguments upon figures derived from the Report issued by the Board of Trade in 1910. This report gives the average weekly wages of agricultural labourers in 1907 as 17s. 6d. Then, added these apologists for low wages, think of the advantages the country labourer has over the town labourer, in being able to obtain cheaper cottages and cheaper food.

I think we have seen enough of these cheaper cottages—with their insidious heritage of disease, involving extra expenditure in sickness, involving extra fuel to dry the reeking-damp walls and floors, and for repairs that often have to be performed by the tenants' own hands—to regard them as anything but cheap; but we will turn at once to examine official figures concerning the labourer's wage.

Averages are all very well for Blue Books, but when you come to tell the agricultural labourer of Norfolk, or of Suffolk, or of Bedfordshire, or of Cambridgeshire, or of Oxfordshire, or of Northamptonshire, or of Huntingdonshire, or of Berkshire, or of Sussex, or of Wiltshire, or of Dorsetshire, or of Gloucestershire, that the average wages of the agricultural labourer throughout England are 17s. 6d., he will answer, "That may be so, but I know it is not *my* average wage"; and you cannot expect the man living on wages below the average to derive much satisfaction from a statement of averages beyond his reach.

The official returns, which include all extra earnings and allowances in kind, give the average earnings per week of ordinary labourers in these southern and eastern counties as only 16s. a week. Low as this figure is, I place it as too high a sum in cash equivalent. I do not say that the labourers do not earn this sum; they may earn this and a good deal more, but they do not get it. That was what the labourer felt when he was dragged before the bench of magistrates for snaring a rabbit, and was asked what he earned.

15

" I earns about 24s. a week," stoutly declared Hodge.

" Nonsense, man!" said the magistrate. " What are your wages ? "

" Oh, my wages," he replied, " they be only 12 bob, but I earns 24."

Now how is the Board of Trade Report made up which brings the average of agricultural labourers all over England up to 17s. 6d. ? The information is based entirely on the figures given, not by the labourers, but by their employers. I am not going to dispute these figures, as far as the cash wages are concerned, though it is important to note that they do not include the earnings of " odd men or casual men." But what I wish to point out is that the sums placed by farmers to their credit for allowances in kind are of very doubtful cash value. It is only human nature that all farmers, desiring to appear as generous as possible, should put down sums against allowances in kind which are very far from being accurate. Indeed I doubt whether Farmer Giles, goose-quill in hand, who perhaps has never had an account-book to keep during his whole life, would retain anything like accurate figures in his head as to the cash equivalent of many of these " allowances."

And what are these allowances in kind?
They include such items as "free house,
garden, potato ground (or potatoes), allotments, fuel (or fuel carted) meal, milk, or
other food, straw for pigs, and even beer or
cider." These items are beside cash payments for "piece work, hay and corn harvest,
overtime, Michaelmas money, journey money,
land money, or any other money payments."

Surely only a middle-class bureaucracy
could be mean enough to take into account a
gallon or two of beer, a truss or two of straw,
a bag of potatoes, a bucket of separated
milk, or a bundle or two of faggots—often a
gift of charity on the part of a farmer—as
part payment of a labourer's wage. Imagine
a schedule being drawn up of the average
earnings of managing directors of City companies in which invitations to a champagne
lunch, a box of expensive cigars, a barrel of
oysters, a first-class season ticket, a first-class
cabin on an ocean liner, all given for business
purposes, were taken into account!

Wet days too, which recur with such
lamentable frequency in our unfortunate
climate for the thousands of field-labourers
who are only casual hands, bring real averages
down with a run; but these do not enter into
the compilations of farmers. There are thousands of casual men at work on our farms,

They get few or no allowances in kind, and their wages, when rain, sleet, frost, and snow do not interrupt their labours, are paid for at the munificent rate of from two to three shillings a day.

Probably the wages of these men do not average more than 10s. a week, which means that their families must have to live partly upon public or private charity. It also means that their children are invariably ill-nourished, and in insanitary cottages easily become victims to diphtheria or tuberculosis.

In the very interesting and informative paper prepared by Mr. H. H. Mann for the Sociological Society, called *Life in an Agricultural Village in England*, the average earnings published by the Board of Trade are searchingly questioned by him. Mr. Mann made a most thorough investigation of one village in Bedfordshire, that of Ridgmount. He has not taken a few selected farmers all over the kingdom, such as was done in the case of the Board of Trade, but has taken the earnings of every household in one village. Instead of an average of 16s. 2d., which is the Board of Trade figure for Bedfordshire, Mr. Mann's very thorough enquiry yields an average of only 14s. 4d. Moreover, if foremen be excluded, he finds the average wages paid in a village amount to 13s. 7½d. per head per week for his 65 agricultural labourers who are working at full rates. The extras amount to only another 8½d. The extras perhaps come to a smaller amount than in some surrounding villages, because the Duke of Bedford pays in many departments as high a wage as 15s. a week, and this munificent sum carries with it no extras. The standard of other farmers is 12s. to 14s. a week, but these give a few more extras. Mr. Mann has been careful to exclude from his table all old labourers and youths who were not earning a man's full wage.

With the inclusion of the foreman Mr. Mann brings the average earnings up to 14s. 11d. per week, a sum very considerably below that obtained by Mr. Wilson Fox.

" I cannot help thinking," states Mr. Mann, " that in working out his averages he (Mr. Fox) has not allowed enough for the enormously greater number of the lower grade of labourers over higher grades ; and I think if this were taken into account his figures will not be very different from mine."

Now Mr. Mann's investigations show that over one third—34·3 per cent.—of the whole population of the village was without the means of sustaining life in a state of mere physical efficiency according to Mr. Rowntree's standard ; and the percentage rises to no less than 41 when the working class alone are concerned.

" The life-history of the average farm hand,"
remarks Mr. C. R. Buxton in his admirable paper
in the *Contemporary Review*, August 1912, " with
no other resources than his earnings as a labourer,
was traced by Mr. Mann, so far as its material environment is concerned, with the utmost accuracy.
We learn that the labourer first rises above the
poverty-line when he begins, or a sufficient number
of his brothers begin, to earn wages. He can secure
sufficient food, clothing, and shelter until he is a
married man and has two children. Then he again
sinks below the line and does not rise above it a
second time till most of his children have left school
and begun to earn wages. Ere long the young
wage-earners begin to leave home ; old age draws
on ; the second period of prosperity is over, and he
crosses the poverty-line once more, never to emerge
again above it."

Mr. Buxton's own personal investigations
as to the average rate of labourers' wages in
Oxfordshire are illuminating. He writes :

I have recently been down into Northamptonshire and Oxfordshire, and I found there that in
many of the villages the wages of the agricultural
labourers were 10s., 11s., and 12s. per week, and
they have to lose time in wet weather. Hundreds
of them have gone home at the week-end during
the winter months with only 8s. for the week.
The general statement made to me, which I can
bear out by experience, is that the average earnings
of those labourers does not amount to more than
12s. per week. Now, if you will kindly allow me,
I will show what this will come to per meal. Take
a man with a wife and three children, and deduct

the following items of expenditure from his wages, which must be deducted before the question of food can be dealt with. I find the rents of cottages average 2s. 6d. per week; a hundredweight of coal is necessary, and that is 1s. 4d.; the man's club is 6d., and clothing, etc., 9d. That means 5s. 1d. to be deducted from his wages, and that will leave 6s. 11d. for food for the family. With a family of five, they will require 105 meals in the week; ¾d. per meal would amount to 6s. 6¾d., so there is a balance of 4¼d. left out of the 12s.!

The conditions that Mr. Buxton found in Oxfordshire I have found in other counties, notably in Gloucestershire, and yet if we turn to the Board of Trade figures we shall find that it gives the average earnings of labourers in Oxfordshire at 16s. 4d., and in Gloucestershire at 17s. 1d. " In Somersetshire," writes a *Daily News* correspondent on September 9, 1912, " wages vary between 11s. and 12s. a week." In some of the villages near East Coker one hears of wages as low as 9s. a week being paid, and near Martock one finds an overtime rate of 6d. for three hours in harvest time. In the Ilchester district 11s. and 12s. are the general rate. Now let us turn to the Board of Trade Returns. The average earnings are placed at 17s. 8d.!

Again, these Returns show the average earnings of Essex labourers to be as high as 17s. 7d., and yet in a reply that I received to a letter of mine in the *Westminster Gazette* it will be seen that a large farmer in Essex gives the weekly earnings of the regular men, in cash, "as near 16s. per week as possible." I print the letter here in full:

ORANGE HALL,
GOSFIELD, ESSEX.
July 4, 1912.

DEAR SIR,—I am not in the habit of writing letters to the papers, but your extraordinary letter in last night's *Westminster* I feel ought to be replied to, and I therefore write you personally.

On about 1,000 acres of land that I farm, I find my wages bill for last year amounts to £1,650, and I employ regularly just over 30 men (to-day have 34, and 3 boys) and some extra labour occasionally. I find the average weekly earnings of my regular men during the past twelve months, *in cash*, is as near 16s. per week as possible. Nothing is put down for cheap cottages and garden: many pay under 2s. per week for cottage and garden sufficient to grow all vegetables required. Nearly all the young men have bicycles to ride, and the families of the older men, both boys and girls, have their own bicycles. I don't think I am given credit for paying higher wages than my neighbours. I simply let my own case speak for itself, and shall be quite willing to show you or anyone interested my labour books.

Yours truly,
(*Signed*) ALFRED BLOMFIELD.
Mr. F. E. GREEN.

This gentleman, naturally enough, wishing to appear as good a paymaster as possible,

states that his own regular men only earn
16s. a week, a sum which includes all cash
payments for harvest money, etc., and yet
the Board of Trade Returns place the average
earnings as high as 17s. 7d.

Now let us examine the purchasing power
of these poor wages. Mr. Buxton has given
a labourer's budget from Oxfordshire. I will
give one sent to me by a Wiltshire labourer
whose regular earnings were 12s. a week.

How the 12s. a week was spent one week:

		s.	d.
Bread, 6 gallons at 11d.	. .	5	6
Salt butter, 2 lb. at 11d.	. .	1	10
Lard, 1 lb.	. . . . .	0	6
Bacon	. . . . .	1	0
Tea, ½ lb.	. . . . .	0	6
Sugar, 4 lb.	. . . . .	1	0
Rice, 2 lb.	. . . . .	0	4
Milk	. . . . . .	0	6
Soap	. . . . . .	0	3
Starch	. . . . .	0	1
Oil, 2 qts.	. . . . .	0	6
		12	0

Boots ⎫
Clothing ⎬ To be paid for out of extra work of
Rent ⎭ harvest, which sometimes brings in
about £3.

To this statement my friend adds :

Three meals a day for 8 people for 1 week =
168 meals; 12s. to pay for the food is 144 pence,

that is, less than a penny to pay for a meal for a working man, to say nothing about a pint of ale or a pipe of tobacco.

Some weeks the 12s. would be spent slightly different—perhaps a shilling's worth of butcher's cuttings instead of bacon or other things: a little different, but the total would be much the same, and anyone would be a clever chap if he could show how I can save fourpence a week to pay into a club for sickness.

We wonder how many townsmen who write of this delectable life on 12s. a week would like to live it in its entirety for fifty-two weeks in a year. How on earth boots, rent, and clothing are to be purchased out of the harvest money remains to me a mystery!

It is a common error of townsmen to assume that the cost of living is lower in the country. There are only two things that are cheaper in the country than in the town: and those two things are houses and fuel, and of these fuel is often cheaper in the town. It is only cheaper in woodland districts, and even here the open fireplaces, in which alone wood can be properly burned, have given place to kitcheners; and coal is invariably dearer in the village, owing to the extra cost of carriage, than in the neighbouring country town. Vegetables are certainly cheaper if the labourer has a good garden or allotment on which to produce them, but

if he be denied these he often has to pay as
much for vegetables and fruit as any townsman. He will indeed have to buy from the
coster who brings out from the great market-
places of London, Birmingham, and Manches-
ter the very things that the labourer has
produced in the fields. A perpetual cascade
of milk flows from the country into the large
towns ; heavily laden wagons and trucks
bear fruit and vegetables from the countryside into the town. The labourer has produced them certainly, but he tastes but
little of them ; they are sold to him as a
favour at top retail prices !

In what way does the labourer's wife
possess a greater purchasing power with the
meagre wages of her husband than her poorly
paid sister in the towns ? For clothing,
drapery, grocery, and butcher's meat she has
invariably to pay a higher price ; and those
who have any knowledge of the little village
shop where bootlaces, oranges, flannelette, and
margarine jostle one another for supremacy
in the little window, will know how shoddy
are the goods meted out for sale to the
labourers by the large wholesale houses. It
is to the country villages that the travellers
take the goods unsaleable in the town. Anyone who has had a lodging in the one spare
bedroom over a village shop will know how

salt and fat has been the bacon, how rancid the butter, how poisonous the tea, and how ineffectual the coffee.

It is a very dangerous thing to catalogue the prices of shop-goods. Those critics with long noses but small minds, ever on the track to sniff trifling inaccuracies and expose them to the world with a gesture of profound wisdom, are sure to be close on my heels yapping out about some cheapjack of theirs with lower prices.

I am willing, however, to take my chance, and publish figures that have been searchingly scanned by one who was once a London grocer, and is now a tiller of the soil.

These are the prices which the labourer's wife has to pay for goods in her own village, compared with the prices paid for goods of the same quality in the nearest country town nine miles away:

	Village Grocer.		The Town Stores.
Bread, quartern	6d.	.	5d. & 6d.
Cheese (lb.) .	8d.	.	6½d.
Sugar (lb.) .	2½d.	.	2d.
Flour (stone) .	1s. 9d.	.	1s. 6d.
Candles (pkt.)	10d.	.	8½d.
Oil (gallon) .	9d.	.	7d.
Bacon (lb.) .	11d.	.	9½d.
Jam (2 lb.) .	9d.	.	7½d.
Butter (lb.) .	1s. 2d.	.	1s.
Macaroni (lb.)	5d.	.	3d.

These figures show that the cost of groceries alone is 20 per cent. more in the little village shop than in a large town store. Indeed there is little need to prove this to middle-class people who live in the country, for they invariably receive a weekly box of provisions from Harrods or the Army and Navy Stores. They would tell you that they cannot afford to shop locally.

On a Saturday night the little wayside country station is often crowded with the wives of labourers, sometimes accompanied by their husbands, taking the train to the nearest country town. They will tell you that it pays them to expend a shilling on a railway fare in order to obtain the lower town prices on the goods. It seems hard, though, that the labourer's wife should be forced to trudge home many miles heavily laden, through the lack of efficient and cheap distribution agencies. It certainly does not point to living being cheaper in the country.

Indeed, it seems that those who are responsible for the government of this country have, with extraordinary self-abnegation, determined that the labourer of the field shall have his journey to heaven unimpeded by many possessions, whilst their own journey thither shall be made the more strenuous by many encumbrances fashioned of gold.

Poverty, though, can cast many a shadow and open many a pit, for him who has to tread the way with hobnailed boots. Yet it is extraordinary what virtues those who labour with their hands for small wages are supposed to possess.

It is really splendid how, under the most adverse circumstances conceivable, labourers do manage to bring up their families to be useful and decent citizens. I know of an old Norfolk labourer, over seventy years of age, who has been working an allotment for over six years, who has brought up three families in a cottage with only one bedroom, divided for decency with a sheet hung across the middle of the room. Yet five of his six girls have turned out well, and his five boys are all clean-living working men. Only one of them (who has become a fisherman) shows any signs of being the least unsteady, and that only when he comes home at the end of a season. Besides adding to England's industrial workers in a generous way, this old man produced in 1912 £74 worth of fruit from his allotment !

Many a time have I had to listen to stories of lives that drink brings to a tragic end in my own village—the drink that is poured down the throat of thirsty labourers by their employers to speed on the day's work, the drink that is offered at every turn near the gates of every large country house for some slight service performed, the drink that flows from the cellars of the rich between elections and that flows from the taproom of the public house so generously before an election, paid for by some " unknown gentleman."

" It is dreadful," said a lady once to me, " how the men in our village do drink."

" And yet," I replied, " you invariably support the party that is most interested in the expansion of the liquor traffic."

It *is* dreadful : because those who have daily to lift feet so heavily weighted with clay, have also to carry poor brains heavily drugged by alcohol.

But the poor, at any rate, manfully bear their share in our national vice ; they suffer the penalty of loss of Church charities, or of loss of employment. On the other hand the rich, with lordly indifference to financial results, can swagger as they ride drink-sodden to their doom.

I was acquainted with a Master of Foxhounds who was rarely seen sober in the saddle. Yet this did not seem to deter any lady in the district from asking him to dinner or to a ball. I was also acquainted with his estate carpenter, whom he discharged for being drunk. The income of the Master of Foxhounds, instead of diminishing, increased with the rise of land values. The income of the carpenter steadily decreased. I traced him eventually, sunk in the depths of despair, fighting the wolf at the door of a suburban slum.

When wages are very low it is no wonder that labourers, and their wives as well, laugh to scorn the gospel of thrift and snatch at any passing pleasure that seems to bring colour into their drab lives. They are quick to note that in the houses of the rich, whatever else wealth may be, it is certainly not "the wages of abstinence." Can they take friends into their one sitting-room, which is kitchen, nursery, and sometimes bedroom combined? The taproom of the village inn, where there is room to stretch their legs, is the only place open to them to show hospitality.

I shall be told that the lure of the town, with its lighted streets, its music-halls, its cinematograph shows, will always triumph over the joys of any rustic civilisation we may like to vision; but what of those thousands of countrymen who have trod with weary feet the unyielding pavements of our cities and become disillusioned? Stronger than the call of the return to nature to the cultured is the earth-hunger of the children of the soil.

A young Irish writer, a weaver of romances, told me he met a boy about to leave school in one of the most beautiful glens of Antrim.

" What are you going to do when you leave school ? " he said to the boy.

" I am going to see life," he answered. " I am going to Glasgow, where I have a brother-in-law who is a potman." And he mentioned one of the worst streets in that overcrowded northern metropolis.

This story illustrates in a graphic way what many townsmen are constantly telling me. The sole solution of the rural exodus to the music-hall-intoxicated mind is more music-halls. Lord Salisbury was, I think, the statesman who suggested travelling circuses. There is something to commend in this classical palliative. A well-organised State circus is only to be seen now when a king is crowned. The Board of Education, or perhaps the Board of Agriculture, which also indulges in fisheries, might effectively teach a race, whose political vision seems circumscribed by the beat of the parish constable, some idea of their Imperial greatness.

Lord Lansdowne and Mr. Bonar Law might do worse than embody this in the programme of rural reform : animals drawn from all our distant dependencies—elephants from India, kangaroos from Australia, lions

16

from South Africa, bears from Canada. These, brought in captivity before Hodge's eyes, must surely dazzle him with a sense of his Imperial greatness abroad—however sorry a figure he may cut at home. Though herded like sheep in a pen, at the sound of the lion's roar he may arch his neck and thrill with sensation at the echo of the Imperial voice.

Personally I do not believe the music-hall has any great attraction for the countryman. The rustle of electric trams, the blaze of brilliantly lighted streets, the blare of the music-hall, the flash of the cinematograph, are things to be seen, to be felt, to be heard once in a way. They visit these scenes as sight-seers, just as the educated classes from quiet English cathedral towns visit Chicago or New York—to gaze at some awful monstrosity. Both the cathedral townsman and the country yokel experience a thrill of pleasurable excitation, but neither wishes to stay or live within the zone of the alien, bizarre environment.

You would think that a man who could turn his hand to any kind of manual labour, whose throat burns with an unquenchable thirst, would stay where public-houses are as thick as mushrooms on an autumn pasture. Such a man has constantly worked for me. His one joy in life, beside his love for contact with the living earth, is to get drunk. But instead of living on the outskirts of the slum area he lives in a shed in the middle of a field two miles from the nearest public-house, which he is not allowed to enter. He once left his job of trimming my hedges to drive to London—over thirty miles—with a coster friend : the coster wanted to end up the day's debauch at a music-hall ; but the countryman would have none of the music-hall. It had no interest for him. It spoke a language he did not understand.

I asked another man who was working for me if he had ever been to London. " Yes, once," he answered. " I took some holly Christmas time to the Borough market." And he told me he had slept on the wagon nearly all the way. He evinced no desire to return to the metropolis. What he saw of the fruit and the vegetables in the Borough market interested him more than other sights foreign to his eyes.

A boy of sixteen who works for me was recently taken, with other youths belonging to a wood-carving class, to London, and was shown over the cathedral, the museums, and the picture-galleries. When he returned I could get nothing out of him about what he had seen except that he saw some armour which had been stored away for " a donkey's number of years." The one thing he did speak about that had made a vivid impression on him was the skilful handling of the reins of the driver of the wagonette amid the crowded streets of London ! *That* was a part of the life he understood.

Town civilisation and rural civilisation are two different things—a fact which it is difficult for townsmen to appreciate. The old peasant civilisation of England was destroyed when by Enclosure Acts the keystone of the arch was knocked out, and those who teach in our elementary schools have unfortunately helped in this work of destruction. The children soon assimilate bourgeoisie ideals from teachers who have often been the clever Sunday-school scholars veneered with gentility, and learn, from the constant exhortations to look up to their "betters," to despise the status of their fathers.

There is little or no attempt to teach the children of the heroic struggles for freedom of their forbears. No history is unveiled to them such as we find in the eloquent places of *The Village Labourer*, by J. L. and Barbara Hammond. No picture is put in front of them of the winning back of a rustic civilisation, a civilisation not superimposed from the towns, but something evolved from the noble clay under their feet and out of the wood resounding with the echo of the axe.

We have had in the past a vision of an artisan civilisation in the Guilds of the Middle Ages. And we have to-day, in the most poverty-stricken parts of Arcadia within the British Isles, a glimpse into the revival of a rustic civilisation. Amid the bogs of Ireland, in County Council Institutes, the arts and crafts woven and hammered out of the plastic earth and its products are applied to peasant life.

The Irish are stimulated by the pride of race and the love of country, a pride and a love almost obliterated in our English peasantry by the passing of the Enclosure Acts. Besides, there is a community of interests amongst the Irish peasants : they are nearly all little farmers, living in the same stratum of society. In England the large farmer is ever menacing any attempt of the labourer to combine socially or politically to obtain a fuller life.

The English farmer knows full well that there is often little to distinguish him in culture from his farm servant. In the early years of their youth they probably both attended the same National school. That very fact, instead of making the farmer more humanly disposed towards his servant, seems to accentuate his desire for deference

to be shown to him by his employees. He
knows, too, that many of his men, if given the
land and the capital, could farm better than
himself. Unlike the Irish farmer, who has
always looked upon the landlord as the enemy,
the English farmer regards the landlord as his
co-partner. He is bound to him by a tie of
sinister affection. The labourer must be kept
in his place.

It is not trying to better your own individual
position that is resented so much by the master
class as trying to better the position of your
fellows. Take, for instance, the case of the
present chairman of the Parish Council of
Potter Heigham in Norfolk. He organised
and acted as secretary of a branch of a
Labourers' Union. He did this so well that
the farmers had to raise wages for a year or
two, but, by degrees, insidiously, they got rid
of the union men one by one, replacing them
with men from another county, seducing
those that were left by giving them favoured
jobs. Finally they smashed up the union.
Then they refused to employ the secretary,
and during the following winter and spring he
was denied a stroke of work for twenty-two
weeks. He could get very little to do during
two years of a venomous boycott. Access to
the land, however, gave him a firmer foothold
on life, and now he works a small holding of

The courageous man who was refused work for twenty-two weeks for starting a branch of a Labourers' Union where wages are only 12s. a week. He is now chairman of the Parish Council, Potter Heigham.

To face page 246.

six acres of fruit and ploughed land, and rents a piece of the marsh. He keeps a horse, a couple of cows, some pigs and chickens, and does a fair amount of carting for his neighbours.

It is not labourers only who have to endure a life spent under the patriarchal power exercised by the farmers. I have known of farmers' sons who felt the parental yoke so galling that they have emigrated, and some have even preferred to become shop-assistants in country towns rather than work on the farm. On the farm their hours of labour were interminable, and, unless completely out of sight of their father's eye, they might be called upon to do some piece of farm drudgery at any moment.

At the present moment I know of a farmer's son who is working as a roadman rather than on his father's farm. He told me that work on that farm meant slavery without an hour of leisure. I know, too, of a farmer, an old man with a long grey beard, who rides his well-groomed horse around his many broad acres daily, and is worth, I am told, £30,000. He keeps his three sons hoeing a field of turnips amidst a gang of labourers. You may hear that a farmer has put his sons into certain homesteads dotted about his own large farm, but it does not really mean that the sons are now master men. They are often merely paid hands. The sons are put there to prevent the farm being taken for small holdings. Each son in occupation is put down in the rate-books as a separate farmer, although the father secretly pays the whole amount of rent and rates, as well as takes the profits.

In spite of all the forces of oppression, there is more hope of evolving a finer civilisation from cottage homes than from tenements around which factory chimneys daily belch forth their impurities. The factory hand has little interest in performing the monotonous routine of his daily task. The agricultural labourer, on the other hand, is still wedded to the love of the earth. He still, in spite of task-masters, takes a pride in his work. This will largely account for the fact, so puzzling to cultured city minds, that a labourer will prefer to work for a hard master who can understand, and sometimes appreciate, his work, than for a refined, sympathetic townsman-employer who rarely glances at the man's work, and when he does cannot understand the difficulties with which the labourer has had to contend, or the skill with which he has executed the work.

" I ain't satisfied with this bit o' mowing

to-day," has a homeless, beer-drenched labourer sometimes said to me; "I believe I could a' done it better with a clasp-knife." And he would remain sullenly indignant with himself for the rest of the day because his work was not done well.

What, however, rankles in the mind of the labourer, if he be a farm servant living in a farm-tied cottage, is being asked very often to work hours and hours overtime without any extra payment; and when extra payment is given for overtime it rarely exceeds 3*d.* an hour, the price meted out to a sweated woman worker in big towns.

I think I have established beyond a shadow of doubt that agricultural labour is a sweated industry; that the labourer, his wife, and his children have to live upon means inadequate to sustain them in either physical or mental efficiency.

A bold stroke of statesmanship can alone save our countryside from being denuded of brain-stuff and manual labour. A few kind-hearted employers here and there, trying to raise wages, soon find to their cost that they rouse the animosity of the entire countryside, which seems suddenly to swarm with hostile farmers.

A friend of mine some time ago raised the wages of the men on his farm in Norfolk

by only one shilling a week, and yet he was
deliberately accused by an adjoining landowner of "setting class against class," and
the scowls with which he was accosted by
his farming neighbours, on his way to play
the organ in church, gave him a glimpse of
the strange idea of Christian brotherhood
possessed by those who spent their lives
in buying and selling bullocks. It was
only this year that Mr. F. J. C. Montagu, of
Lindford Hall, Norfolk, on deciding to pay
his married labourers 17s. per week, and his
single labourers 15s., in place of the current
wages of 12s. or 13s., evoked a hostile protest from the tenant farmers in the *Eastern
Daily Press*.

Without further legislation the agricultural labourer could be scheduled under the
Trade Boards Act and a minimum wage
instituted ; but in the formation of these
Boards the area selected should be very
large, for there is no reason why the farmer
of Norfolk and Suffolk should not pay as
high wages as the farmers in Derbyshire and
Northumberland. Indeed they ought to pay
better wages, for the soil they till is some of
the finest in England. The difference in wages
lies solely in the proximity to mines and
other industrial centres. The area governed
by each Board must be large, too, to avoid

the parochial tyranny which, as I have shown, is constantly brought into play with regard to cottages and allotments. The Cotswold labourer, though afraid to meet the Cotswold farmer, would not be afraid to bargain with the great sheep-farmers of the Downs.

To effectually stem the tide of the rural exodus is not only a matter of giving high wages, important as this is ; it is not only a matter of a better supply of cottages, free of the tyranny of landlordism ; it is not only a question of obtaining access to land. The vital determinant is the human treatment of the labourer ; his social status. With this I will deal in my next and last chapter.

CHAPTER XI

THE REVOLT

I HAVE shown the sinister way in which the tyranny of the countryside differs from that of the town. When the town worker shuts the factory gates behind him he walks the streets a free citizen. In the country it is deplorably different. When the labourer shuts his employer's farm gate behind him, he leaves but to enter his employer's cottage as a tenant. His leisure hours are spent almost entirely under his employer's eye. On the allotments, in the pheasant-haunted lane, in the public-house, in the club-room, or in the Council-room, he is at all times under the eye of his employer or his employer's friends, and if he be in debt to the village grocer he remains chained to the land like an indentured slave. He has become the most patronised, the most tyrannised over of all the peasants of Europe.

Cut off from daily contact with his fellows, the mind-destroying isolation of the labourer

The isolation of the rural worker. So large is the field sometimes in which he works entirely alone that he brings his dinner to the middle of the field near his work.

To face page 253.

reduces him to a thrall. The farm work, that keeps the labourer from sunrise to sunset working alone in a field with nothing but crows to keep him company, may be necessary; but there is no necessity to keep him chained to a house adjoining the byres and at a long distance from his fellows, whom he may see but once or twice a week, and whom his wife rarely sees at all. This isolation is the deadly blight that renders the labourer so slow of speech, and limits his political as well as his social horizon. He is, I repeat, the worst used and the least bold peasant in Europe.

It is futile to assert that the French peasant on his own land is poorer and works harder than the English agricultural labourer. Though the French peasant may be in the hands of money-lenders, and though the English small-holder may be robbed by market salesmen and railway companies, each possesses a dignity, a glimpse of freedom unvisioned by the agricultural labourer.

Besides the raising of wages, the granting of access to the land, and the supply of cottages uncontrolled by their masters, the vital determinant to keep the younger generation on the land is the raising of their social status and evolving a finer civilisation.

Rural reformers are unfortunately of that

type so pointedly described by a distinguished modern writer as men "who feel that the cruelty to the poor is a kind of cruelty to animals. *They never feel that it is injustice to equals ; nay, it is treachery to comrades.*"

The children of the agricultural labourer note that their father is despised by the gentry ; that he is bullied by the farmer ; that in the eye of the law he is a social outcast ; that the vicar looks upon him as a kind of Lazarus waiting, cap in hand, outside the vicarage gates ; and that their mother is regarded as a person fit only to perform the most menial services, that are scorned by the servants of the rich.

It is not sufficient that a labourer can become a Parish Councillor merely to stand up like a sheep before his master, a fellow-councillor in the village schoolroom. He must be able to meet him as man to man, without fear of losing both his home and his work.

Does it ever occur to my town reader that for the agricultural labourer there are no holy days, no festivals ; and for the tender of beasts no Sabbath day, no one day of rest in all the three hundred and sixty-five ?

Not a bad record, think you, for thirsty devotees of Bacchus. Bacchus is their only

God of Joy, but we would that they should follow Pan and have ears attuned to catch the sound of his flutings amid the reeds, and the woods, and the wind-swept hills.

We are becoming more alive to the fact that agriculture is not only the most ancient but also the most learned of crafts. It contains worlds of undiscovered country in which our greatest modern scientists are continually delving.

Within our immediate reach is a rustic civilisation, finer than any ever imagined by writers on agricultural reform; and its first lessons should be given in the elementary school, where the children should be taught at an early date the greatness of their fathers' calling, and the divinity of their mothers' work.

Among the finer intelligences of my acquaintance are two men who are both the sons of agricultural labourers. They possess in a high degree that gallantry of mind which carries them far in the world of culture; and yet both of them are the sons of fathers and of mothers who have laboured in the fields, hoeing the turnips that have sometimes been their only meal.

At work from early childhood, for two or three brief years only do the farmer's boy and the servant girl ever enter into the gaiety of life. It is only in his adolescent days that the country swain can afford to break out into bucolic dandyism. It is only when the lass is about to leave service to become his wife that she can lightly tread, amid a froth of cheap lace, to the primrose land. Almost before the sound of the wedding bells dies away, he wears sackcloth on his shoulders, and ties his steaming corduroys around with string; and as for her, she is rarely seen abroad save to taste the tepid joys of a Mothers' Meeting. Muddy roads, the lack of public conveyances, scandalous shoe-leather, the arduous duties of maternity and the increasing domestic drudgery keep her effectually incarcerated. At thirty she is an old woman—the age when the Park Lane matron is blazoning into a gorgeous womanhood. At forty, toothless, she has fully experienced the keen, heroic edge of life, and becomes exhausted by physical weariness. Her one hope is that her children may not live the life that she and her husband have had to live.

The Holy Grail may be found in every labourer's cot, but Sir Galahads, richly caparisoned, daily ride past to enter the gilded gates of the Park.

To uplift those who remain entrapped

within this Slough of Despond, to infuse them with some sense of social solidarity, it may yet be that burgesses, living in the larger freedom of our towns, will ride forth as St. George, to free their fellow-countrymen, to rescue maidens and little children languishing for want of good food, and to slay the dragons that keep them immured within dens of disease.

Probably the symbols of brotherhood borne aloft by the flower of our chivalry will be the banners of working men, members of the great Freemasonry, the Trade Union of our towns. At their last great Congress in September 1912 the craftsmen of the towns at last declared their resolve to march to the aid of the craftsmen of the fields.

Some day, too, perhaps a gaunt army will rise up, some with smocks and some with sackcloth flung over their tattered shirts and steaming corduroys, armed with bill-hooks and pitchforks, followed by haggard, fierce-eyed women, and little children with faces filled with wonderment and fear at the Great Adventure. On all their lips will be the words of the one revolutionary book with which they are familiar. They will cry aloud to the Lord of Battles to put down the mighty from their seat and exalt those of low degree.

Their entrance upon London, the citadel of the possessing classes, the site of the council-chamber which decides whether their hire shall be worthy of their labour— which decides whether they shall live in rat-riddled hovels or healthy homes—would surely open the eyes of those who have so long remained blind to the writing on the walls of the Temple of Humanity.

The miners suspended the work of the country, arrested the futilities of parliamentarians, and made them not only listen but also act. Why should not the labourers ?

Their sons had been boiled in the factory pot and were being educated at colleges where the history of their struggles for freedom is taught ; sons who, instead of seeking social advancement for themselves, had come back to the village to tell them the gospel of good news of how freedom might be won: how the land that had been stolen from them by Enclosure Acts might be restored if they chose, by the magic of the pen wielded in the great council-chamber.

Vision, then, some four million strong of them, surging along the great arteries which have so long drained the life-blood of the nation, thronging the great North Road, pouring in from the West Country along the Bath Road, swarming along the Romford

Road, marching along the old Roman Road
which still strikes like an arrow from the
sea to the heart of the Empire : all these
streaming hosts converging towards Trafalgar
Square.

Callous clubmen and cold officials become
suddenly warm with the flush of fear or of
sympathy as these mighty lines are joined
by fresh armies of those who once left the
countryside to seek the freedom of the
mines, the great metal roads, and the docks.
These have had their day of disillusion-
ment. Filled with high hopes of freedom,
they found that they had to fight like ravening
wolves at the dock-gates for their daily bread,
had to stand idle at the pit-mouth or on the
great metal roadway, waiting for their just
reward. And now they come to swell the
ranks of their brothers.

The women too are there—the mothers
of our Imperial race. With eyes filled with
the burning shame of having to suckle babes
that die through lack of nourishment, they
sweep down upon the nation's council
house at Westminster.

Surely such a sight would stir the nation
to its depths and make its manhood go
down on its knees to crave their pardon for
years of neglect. Nothing would be compar-
able to it. The great marching of the women

of Paris upon Versailles would pale before it. Visitors to London from the uttermost ends of the earth would gaze wide-eyed from their hotel windows, aghast at the spectacle of the richest Empire of the twentieth century athrob with the fever of an oppressed race. They would witness the mighty host of the producers of the staff of life, boiling in the cauldron of revolt. They would be brought face to face with the world's supreme craftsmen—the givers of their daily bread.

From the dawn of artistic expression the Sower has been the symbol of the Immortal One. On this fecund earth of ours he is the supreme, incomparable craftsman. In his superb gesture art is immortalised. He is the only artist who is indispensable. He is the Resurrection and the Life, and yet we crucify him daily. We imprison him in cells rank with fungoid growth; we feed him with the refuse of the earth: him who scatters the largesse of the golden grain. We put upon him menial labour; we rob him of holy days; we keep him with bent back to his task; and we drug his mind with doctored alcohol. We make of him a social outcast, and show his children that we despise him. We spit upon him in the market place, and in his old age incarcerate him in a barrack, and leave him there until the time comes for him to meet his Creator in whose image he was made. That will then be *our* Day of Judgment. Before the great arraignment, what have we to say?

For EU product safety concerns, contact us at Calle de José Abascal, 56–1°,
28003 Madrid, Spain or eugpsr@cambridge.org.

www.ingramcontent.com/pod-product-compliance
Ingram Content Group UK Ltd.
Pitfield, Milton Keynes, MK11 3LW, UK
UKHW010346140625
459647UK00010B/877